MW00666777

TABE 11 & 12 Math Practice Tests: 250 TABE 11 & 12 Math Questions with Step-by-Step Solutions

TABE 11 & 12 Math Practice Tests: 250 TABE 11 & 12 Math Questions with Step-by-Step Solutions

ISBN-13: 978-0-9998087-1-9
ISBN-10: 0-9998087-1-9

For information on bulk discounts, please contact us at: email@examsam.com

The drawings in this publication are for illustration purposes only. They are not drawn to an exact scale.

TABLE OF CONTENTS

How to Use This Publication

As you work through this study guide, you will notice that Practice Tests 1 and 2 are in workbook format, providing study tips after each question.

The format of the first two practice tests introduces the exam concepts and helps you learn the strategies and formulas that you need to answer all of the types of questions on the actual TABE Math Test.

You can refer back to the formulas and tips introduced in the first two practice tests as you work through the remaining material in the book.

For ease of reference during your study, Practice Tests 3, 4, and 5 are organized by skill area, so you will see all of the number and data questions first, followed by the algebra questions and then the geometry questions.

The answers and solutions for the practice tests are provided at the end of each of the practice exams.

This study guide assumes knowledge of basic math skills, such as addition, subtraction, multiplication, division, percentages, and decimals.

Free Basic Math Review Problems

If you have difficulties with basic math problems or if you have been out of school for a while, you may wish to review our free basic math problems before taking the practice tests in this book.

The free review problems can be found at: www.examsam.com

TABE Practice Math Test 1 with Study Tips

Number and data problems:

1) $-(-5) + 3 = ?$

A) –8
B) –2
C) 2
D) 8

Computations with signed numbers are frequently included on the TABE examination. Many of these types of problems will involve integers. Integers are positive and negative whole numbers. Integers cannot have decimals, nor can they be mixed numbers. In other words, they can't contain fractions. One of the most important concepts to remember when working with signed numbers is that two negative signs together make a positive number. So, when you see a number like – (–2) you have to use 2 in your calculation.

2) What is the largest possible product of two even integers whose sum is 22?

A) 11
B) 44
C) 100
D) 120

You will also see problems that ask you to perform multiplication or division on integers. Some of these problems may ask you to find an integer that meets certain mathematical requirements, like the problem above.

3) What is $^1/_3 \times {}^2/_3$?

A) $^2/_3$
B) $^2/_6$
C) $^2/_9$
D) $^1/_3$

You will see problems on the exam that ask you to multiply fractions. To multiply fractions, you first need to multiply the numerators from each fraction. Then multiply the denominators. The numerator is the number on the top of each fraction. The denominator is the number on the bottom of the fraction.

4) $\frac{1}{5} \div \frac{4}{7} = ?$

A) $\frac{4}{20}$

B) $\frac{7}{20}$

C) $\frac{4}{35}$

D) $\frac{5}{35}$

You will also need to know how to divide fractions for the exam. To divide fractions, invert the second fraction by putting the denominator on the top and numerator on the bottom. Then multiply as indicated for the previous problem.

5) What is $\frac{1}{9}+\frac{9}{27}$?

A) $\frac{12}{27}$

B) $\frac{9}{27}$

C) $\frac{3}{27}$

D) $\frac{10}{36}$

In some fraction problems, you will have to find the lowest common denominator. In other words, before you add or subtract fractions, you have to change them so that the bottom numbers in each fraction are the same. You do this by multiplying the numerator by the same number that you used when multiplying to get the new denominator for the fraction.

6) Simplify: $\frac{12}{27}$

A) $\frac{1}{3}$

B) $\frac{3}{4}$

C) $\frac{3}{9}$

D) $\frac{4}{9}$

You will also need to know how to simplify fractions for your exam. To simplify fractions, look to see what factors are common to both the numerator and denominator. Factoring is like taking a number apart. So, what numbers can we multiply together to get 12? What numbers can we multiply together to get 27?

7) $3\frac{1}{3} - 2\frac{1}{2} = ?$

A) $\frac{1}{3}$

B) $\frac{9}{3}$

C) $\frac{5}{6}$

D) $1\frac{1}{2}$

Mixed numbers are those that contain a whole number and a fraction. Convert the mixed numbers back to fractions first. Then find the lowest common denominator of the fractions in order to solve the problem.

8) $-6 \times 3 - 4 \div 2 = ?$

A) –20
B) –18
C) –2
D) 4

This question tests your knowledge of order of operations. The phrase "order of operations" means that you need to know which mathematical operation to do first when you are faced with longer problems. Remember the acronym PEMDAS. "PEMDAS" means that you have to do the mathematical operations in this order: First: Do operations inside **P**arentheses Second: Do operations with **E**xponents Third: Perform **M**ultiplication and **D**ivision (from left to right) Last: Do **A**ddition and **S**ubtraction (from left to right)

9) $\frac{5 \times (7-4)^2 + 3 \times 8}{5 - 6 \div (4-1)} = ?$

A) –23
B) 23
C) $\frac{23}{1/3}$
D) 46

This is an advanced question on order of operations. Remember PEMDAS: Parentheses – Exponents – Multiplication & Division – Addition & Subtraction

10) Consider a class which has n students. In this class, t% of the students subscribe to digital TV packages. Which of the following equations represents the number of students who do not subscribe to any digital TV package?

A) $100(n - t)$
B) $(100\% - t\%) \times n$
C) $(100\% - t\%) \div n$
D) $(1 - t)n$

> You will have to calculate percentages and decimals on the exam, as well as use percentages and decimals to solve other types of math problems or to create equations. Percentages can be expressed by using the symbol %. They can also be expressed as fractions or decimals.

11) Find the value of x that solves the following proportion: $^{3}/_{6} = {}^{x}/_{14}$

A) 3
B) 6
C) 7
D) 8

> A proportion is an equation with a ratio on each side. In other words, a proportion is a statement that two ratios are equal. $^{3}/_{4} = {}^{6}/_{8}$ is an example of a proportion. We will look at ratios again in the next question.

12) In a shipment of 100 mp3 players, 1% are faulty. What is the ratio of non-faulty mp3 players to faulty mp3 players?

A) 1:100
B) 100:1
C) 1:99
D) 99:1

> Ratios take a group of people or things and divide them into two parts. For example, if you spend two hours studying math for every hour that you spend studying English, you get the ratio 2:1. The number before the colon expresses one subset of the total amount of items. The number after the colon expresses a different subset of the total. In other words, when the number before the colon and the number after the colon are added together, we have the total amount of items.

13) A company purchases cell phones at a cost of x and sells the cell phones at four times the cost. Which of the following represents the profit made on each cell phone?

A) x
B) $3x$
C) $4x$
D) $3 - x$

> You will see problems on the test that ask you to set up mathematical equations from basic information. To set up an equation, read the problem carefully and then express the facts in terms of a mathematical equation. The problem tells us that cell phones sell for four times the cost, so "four times" means that we have to multiply. For this problem, profit is calculated by taking the sales price and subtracting the cost.

14) An internet provider sells internet packages based on monthly rates. The price for the internet service depends on the speed of the internet connection. The chart that follows indicates the prices of the various internet packages.

Price in dollars (P)	10	20	30	40
Gigabyte speed (s)	2	4	6	8

Which equation represents the prices of these internet packages?

A) $P = (s - 5) \times 5$
B) $P = (s + 5) \times 5$
C) $P = 5 \div s$
D) $P = s \times 5$

> To set up a basic equation, remember to read the problem carefully and then express the facts in terms of a mathematical equation. For the question above, divide the dollars by the speed to find the mathematical relationship.

15) What is the mean of the following set of numbers? 1, 2, 3, 4, 5, 5, 8, 8, 9

A) 1
B) 2
C) 5
D) 8

> This is our first data analysis problem. The mean is the same as the arithmetic average. The mean is calculated by adding up the total of the values for a data set and then dividing this total by the number of people or items in the group.

16) Consider this data set: 12, 20, 3, 25, 30, 28, 18. What is the median?

A) 12
B) 13
C) 20
D) 35

> The median is simply the middle value in the data set. Put the numbers in the data set in ascending order (from lowest to highest). The median is the middle number in the ordered set.

Algebra concepts and formulas:

17) Simplify: $| 3 - 6 |$
A) –9
B) –6
C) –3
D) 3

When you see numbers between lines like this $| -5 |$, you are being asked the absolute value. Absolute value means that the number or mathematical result from inside the lines is a positive number. So $| -5 | = 5$

18) $(3x - 2y)^2 = ?$
A) $9x^2 + 4y^2$
B) $9x^2 - 6xy^2 + 4y^2$
C) $9x^2 - 12xy + 4y^2$
D) $9x^2 + 12xy^2 + 4y^2$

Multiplying Polynomials Using the FOIL Method – Polynomials are algebraic expressions that contain integers, variables, and variables which are raised to whole-number positive exponents. You will also see binomial problems on the test. Binomial problems will be in this format: (a + b). Quadratic problems may be in this format: (a + b)(c + d).
Multiply the terms in the parentheses in this order: **F**irst – **O**utside – **I**nside – **L**ast
So, $(a + b)(c + d) = (a \times c) + (a \times d) + (b \times c) + (b \times d)$

19) $(x^2 - x - 6) \div (x - 3) = ?$
A) 2x
B) x – 2
C) x – 2
D) x + 2

You may also need to perform long division on quadratics on the exam. A quadratic expression is simply the product of multiplying two binomials together. You can think of long division of the quadratic as reversing the FOIL operation. In other words, your result will generally be in one of the following formats: (x + y) or (x – y)

20) What is the value of the expression $4x^2 + 2xy - y^2$ when $x = 2$ and $y = -2$?
A) 4
B) 6
C) 8
D) 12

You may be asked to calculate the value of an expression by substituting its values. To solve these problems, put in the numbers stated for *x* and *y* and multiply. In this question, $x = 2$ and $y = -2$. Once you have done the multiplication, do the addition and subtraction.

21) What are two possible values of x for the following equation? $x^2 + 6x + 8 = 0$

A) –2 and –4
B) 2 and 4
C) 6 and 8
D) –2 and –6

> You may see problems on the exam that give you a quadratic equation and ask you to determine possible values for the variables in the expression. If you are asked to find values for variables, such as x or y in a math problem, substitute zero for one variable and then work out an answer. Then substitute zero for the other variable to work out the other possible answer.

22) $\dfrac{\frac{1}{7}}{\frac{x}{3}} = ?$

A) $\dfrac{7x}{3}$

B) $\dfrac{3}{7x}$

C) $\dfrac{x}{21}$

D) $\dfrac{21}{x}$

> When you see fractions containing fractions, remember to treat the line that separates the main numerator and main denominator as the division sign. Then invert the second fraction and multiply. To invert, you swap the positions of the numerator and denominator.

23) If $\dfrac{30}{\sqrt{x^2 - 75}} = 6$, then x = ?

A) 100
B) 30
C) 25
D) 10

> You may see fractions that contain radicals in the numerator or denominator. If your problem has a fraction that contains a radical in its numerator or denominator, you need to eliminate the radical by multiplying both sides of the equation by the radical.

24) $\frac{x^5}{x^2 - 6x} + \frac{5}{x} = ?$

A) $\frac{4 + x^6}{x^2 - 3x}$

B) $\frac{4x^2 - 16x}{x^7}$

C) $\frac{x^5 + 5x + 30}{x^2 - 6x}$

D) $\frac{x^5 + 5x - 30}{x^2 - 6x}$

Rational expressions are fractions that contain polynomial expressions. To add or subtract two rational expressions, you need to calculate the lowest common denominator, just like you would for any other problem with fractions. In this problem, x is common to both denominators, so we can convert the denominator of the second fraction to the LCD by multiplying it by $(x - 6)$.

25) $11^5 \times 11^3 = ?$

A) 11^8

B) 11^{15}

C) 22^8

D) 121^8

You will need to know properties of exponents for the examination. You will see questions on the exam that involve adding and subtracting exponents. When the base numbers are the same and you need to multiply the base numbers, you add the exponents. When the base numbers are the same and you need to divide, you subtract the exponents.

26) $x^4 \times x^2 = ?$

A) x^2

B) x^4

C) x^6

D) x^8

You also add the exponents when multiplying base numbers that have the same variable, as in this problem.

27) $10^6 \div 10^4 = ?$

A) 10^{24}

B) 10^2

C) 20^{24}

D) 20^2

Remember to subtract the exponents when you divide the base numbers.

Although not needed for these problems, you may also need to know the following exponent properties for the exam.

Zero exponent: Any number to the power of zero is equal to 1.

Example: $9^0 = 1$

Negative exponents: Remove the negative sign on the exponent by expressing the number as a fraction, with 1 as the numerator. Then place the number with the exponent in the denominator.

Example: $x^{-2} = \frac{1}{x^2}$

Fractional exponents: Place the base number inside the radical sign. The denominator of the exponent is the nth root of the radical. The numerator is the new exponent.

Example: $x^{3/7} = (\sqrt[7]{x})^3$

28) In the equations below, x represents the cost of one online game and y represents the cost of one movie ticket. If $x - 2 > 5$ and $y = x - 2$, then the cost of 2 discounted movie tickets is greater than which one of the following?

A) $x - 2$
B) $x - 5$
C) $y + 5$
D) 10

Inequality problems will have a less than or greater than sign. When solving inequality problems, isolate integers before dealing with any fractions. Also remember that if you multiply an inequality by a negative number, you have to reverse the direction of the less than or greater than sign.

29) $\frac{2x^3}{5} \times \frac{4}{x^2} = ?$

A) $\frac{8x}{5}$
B) $\frac{5}{8x}$
C) $\frac{8}{5}$
D) $8x$

To multiply rational expressions, multiply the numerator of the first fraction by the numerator of the second fraction to get the new numerator. Then multiply the denominators together to get the new denominator. Finally, use exponent laws to simplify the terms in the numerator and denominator.

30) $\frac{6x+6}{x^2} \div \frac{3x+3}{x^3} = ?$

A) $2x$
B) $6x$
C) $8x$
D) $18x^3$

In order to divide rational expressions, invert the second fraction and multiply. Then cancel out any common factors. Be sure to cancel out completely.

31) How many solutions exist for the following equation? $x^2 + 8 = 0$

A) 0
B) 1
C) 2
D) 4

You will see questions on the exam that give you an equation and then ask you how many solutions there are for the equation provided. You will need to consider both positive and negative numbers as potential solutions.

32) How many solutions exist for the following equation? $x^2 - 9 = 0$

A) 0
B) 1
C) 2
D) 3

When you see problems containing x^2 or y^2, remember that any real number squared will always equal a positive number.

33) A company sells jeans and T-shirts. *J* represents jeans and *T* represents T-shirts in these equations: $2J + T = \$50$ and $J + 2T = \$40$. Sarah buys one pair of jeans and one T-shirt. How much does she pay for her entire purchase?

A) \$10
B) \$20
C) \$30
D) \$40

Several questions on the TABE Test will ask you to solve practical problems. Practical problems may involve calculating prices or discounts for items in a store. Other common practical problems involve calculations with exam scores or other data for a class of students.

34) Solve the following by elimination. $x + 4y = 30$

$$2x + 2y = 36$$

A) $x = 2$ and $y = 7$
B) $x = 4$ and $y = 14$
C) $x = 14$ and $y = 4$
D) $x = 16$ and $y = 4$

When you have to solve a problem by elimination, you will see two equations as in this question. In order to solve by elimination, you need to subtract the second equation from the first equation. Put one equation below the other to subtract. Remember to be careful with the negative signs.

35) If $3x - 2(x + 5) = -8$, then $x = ?$
- A) 1
- B) 2
- C) 3
- D) 5

You will see problems involving solving equations for an unknown variable on the exam. To solve the problem, perform the multiplication on the items in parentheses first. Then eliminate the integers by isolating them to one side of the equation. Finally, perform any other operations to solve for x.

36) What ordered pair is a solution to the following system of equations?

$x + y = 9$

$xy = 20$
- A) (2, 7)
- B) (4, 5)
- C) (3, 6)
- D) (5, 3)

For systems of equations problems, you will see two equations, both of which will contain x and y. In one equation, x and y will be added. In the other equation, x and y will be multiplied. In order to solve systems of equations, look at the equation that contains multiplication first. Then find the factors of the product in the equation to solve the problem.

37) Which of the answers below is equal to the following radical expression? $\sqrt{45}$
- A) $1 \div 45$
- B) $5\sqrt{9}$
- C) $9\sqrt{5}$
- D) $3\sqrt{5}$

Square roots and cube roots are sometimes referred to as radicals. You will need to know how to perform the operations of multiplication and division on square and cube roots. You will also see problems that involve rationalizing and factoring square and cube roots. In order to factor a radical, you need to find perfect squares for factors of the number inside the radical sign. For example: $\sqrt{128} = \sqrt{64 \times 2} = \sqrt{8 \times 8 \times 2} = 8\sqrt{2}$

38) $\sqrt{32} + 2\sqrt{72} + 3\sqrt{18} = ?$
- A) $2\sqrt{16} + 2\sqrt{36} + 3\sqrt{9}$
- B) $5\sqrt{122}$

C) $6\sqrt{122}$

D) $25\sqrt{2}$

You may see advanced problems on radicals involving other operations, such as addition or subtraction.

39) $\sqrt{6} \times \sqrt{5} = ?$

A) $\sqrt{30}$

B) $\sqrt{11}$

C) $6\sqrt{5}$

D) $5\sqrt{6}$

To multiply radicals, multiply the numbers inside the square root signs. Then put this result inside a square root symbol for your answer. For example: $\sqrt{x} \times \sqrt{y} = \sqrt{xy}$

40) Express as a rational number: $\sqrt[3]{\frac{64}{125}}$

A) $\frac{1}{5}$

B) $\frac{4}{5}$

C) $\frac{5}{4}$

D) $\frac{8}{25}$

You may see problems on the exam that ask you to rationalize a number or to express a radical number as a rational number. Perform the necessary mathematical operations in order to remove the radical symbol. This normally involves breaking the numerator and denominator into their factors in order to find the square or cube roots.

Geometry and graphing – problems and formulas:

41) Consider the isosceles triangle in the diagram below.

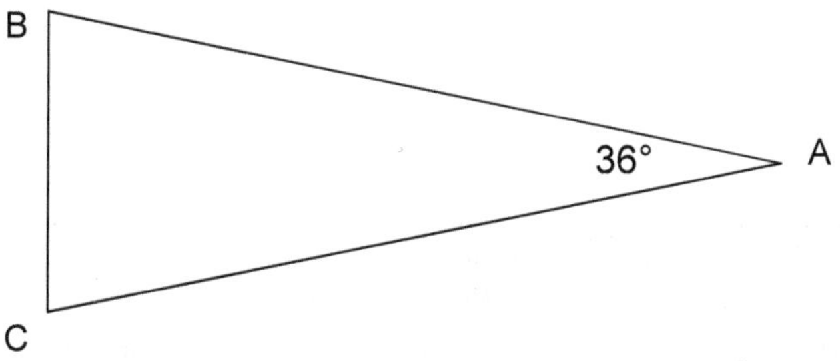

What is the measurement of ∠B?

A) 36°
B) 45°
C) 72°
D) 144°

For angle measurement questions, you need to remember these concepts: (1) The sum of all three angles in a triangle is always 180°; (2) Two sides of an isosceles triangle are equal in length, and their corresponding angles are also equal; (3) For an isosceles triangle, deduct the degrees given from 180° to find out the total degrees of the two other angles.

NOTE: You will see the formulas in this section again when we will look at advanced problems on geometry in the next practice test in this book.

42) A football field is 100 yards long and 30 yards wide. What is the area of the football field in square yards?

A) 130
B) 150
C) 300
D) 3000

You will need to calculate the area of geometric shapes, such as circles, squares, triangles, and rectangles for the test. In this problem, we are working with a rectangle. Be sure that you know how to use these formulas for the exam:

Area of a circle: $\pi \times r^2$ (radius squared)

Area of a square or rectangle: length × width

Area of a triangle: (base × height) ÷ 2

43) If one side of a triangle is 5cm and the other side is 12cm, what is the measurement of the hypotenuse of the triangle?

A) $5\sqrt{12}$ cm

B) $12\sqrt{5}$ cm

C) $\sqrt{17}$ cm

D) 13 cm

The hypotenuse is the side of the triangle that is opposite the right angle. In other words, the hypotenuse is opposite the square corner of the triangle. To calculate the length of the hypotenuse in right triangles, you will need the Pythagorean Theorem. According to the theorem, the length of the hypotenuse (represented by side C) is equal to the square root of the sum of the squares of the other two sides of the triangle (represented by A and B). For any right triangle with sides A, B, and C, you need to remember this formula:

hypotenuse length C = $\sqrt{A^2 + B^2}$

44) In the figure below, XY is 4 inches long and XZ is 5 inches long. What is the area of triangle XYZ?

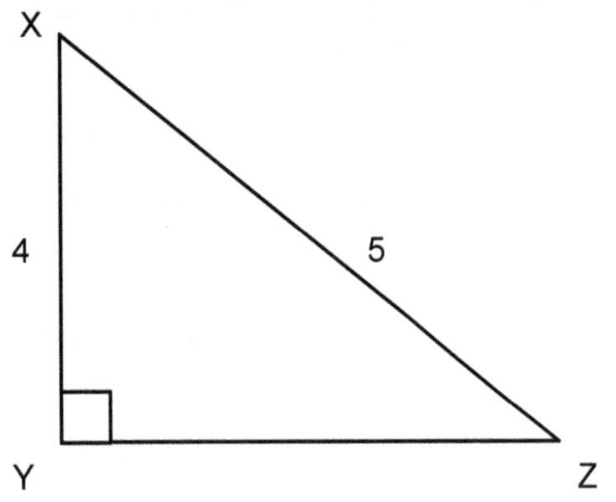

A) 3
B) 5
C) 6
D) 10

Use the Pythagorean Theorem to find the length of YZ.
Then use the formula to calculate the area of a triangle:

triangle area = (base × height) ÷ 2

45) What is the perimeter of a rectangle that has a length of 5 and a width of 3?
A) 15
B) 16
C) 18
D) 40

The perimeter is the measurement along the outer side of a square, rectangle, or hybrid shape. In order to calculate the perimeter of squares and rectangles, you need to use the perimeter formula:

Perimeter = (length × 2) + (width × 2)

46) If a circle has a diameter of 12, what is the circumference of the circle?
A) 6π
B) 12π
C) 24π
D) 36π

The circumference is the measurement around the outside of a circle. You can think of circumference like perimeter, except circumference is used in calculations for circular objects, rather than for shapes like squares or rectangles.

The formula for the circumference of a circle is: Circumference = π × diameter

47) A box is manufactured to contain either laptop computers or notebook computers. When the computer systems are removed from the box, it is reused to hold other items. If the length of the box is 20cm, the width is 15cm, and the height is 25cm, what is the volume of the box?
A) 150
B) 300
C) 750
D) 7500

For the test, you may need to calculate the volume of a cylinder, cone, or rectangular solid.

Rectangular solid volume: base × width × height

Cone volume: $(\pi \times \text{radius}^2 \times \text{height}) \div 3$

Cylinder volume: $\pi \times \text{radius}^2 \times \text{height}$

48) Consider two stores in a town. The first store is a grocery store. The second is a pizza place where customers collect their pizzas after they order them online. The grocery store is represented by the coordinates (−4, 2) and the pizza place is represented by the coordinates (2,−4). If the grocery store and the pizza place are connected by a line segment, what is the midpoint of this line?

A) (1, 1)
B) (−1, −1)
C) (2, 2)
D) (−2, −2)

You may be asked to calculate the midpoint of two points on a graph. Remember that you divide the sum of the two points by 2 because the midpoint is the halfway mark between the two points on the line. The two points are represented by the coordinates (x_1, y_1) and (x_2, y_2). The midpoint of two points on a two-dimensional graph is calculated by using the midpoint formula:

$$(x_1 + x_2) \div 2\ ,\ (y_1 + y_2) \div 2$$

49) Marta runs up and down a hill near her house. The measurements of the hill can be placed on a two dimensional linear graph on which $x = 5$ and $y = 165$. If the line crosses the y axis at 15, what is the slope of this hill?

A) 10
B) 20
C) 30
D) 36

Slope is the measurement of how steep a straight line on a graph is. Slope will be negative when the line slants upwards to the left. On the other hand, slope will be positive when the line slants upwards to the right. The two points are represented by the coordinates (x_1, y_1) and (x_2, y_2). Slope is represented by variable m. We can calculate slope by using the slope formula. The slope formula is as follows:

$$m = \frac{y_2 - y_1}{x_2 - x_1}$$

You will sometimes be given a set of points, and then told where the line crosses the y axis. In that case, you will also need what is known as the slope-intercept formula. In the slope-intercept formula, m is the slope, b is the y intercept (the point at which the line crosses the y axis), and x and y are points on the graph. Here is the slope-intercept formula:

$$y = mx + b$$

50) Find the x and y intercepts of the following equation: $x^2 + 4y^2 = 64$

A) (8, 0) and (0, 4)
B) (0, 8) and (4, 0)
C) (4, 0) and (0, 8)
D) (0, 4) and (8, 0)

You may also be asked to calculate x and y intercepts in geometry problems. The x intercept is the point at which a line crosses the x axis of a graph. In order for the line to cross the x axis, y must be equal to zero at that particular point of the graph. On the other hand, the y intercept is the point at which the line crosses the y axis. So, in order for the line to cross the y axis, x must be equal to zero at that particular point of the graph. For questions about x and y intercepts, substitute 0 for y in the equation provided. Then substitute 0 for x to solve the problem.

TABE Practice Math Test 1 – Answer Key

1) D
2) D
3) C
4) B
5) A
6) D
7) C
8) A
9) B
10) B
11) C
12) D
13) B
14) D
15) C
16) C
17) D
18) C
19) D
20) A
21) A
22) B
23) D
24) D
25) A
26) C
27) B
28) D
29) A
30) A
31) A
32) C
33) C
34) C
35) B

36) B

37) D

38) D

39) A

40) B

41) C

42) D

43) D

44) C

45) B

46) B

47) D

48) B

49) C

50) A

TABE Practice Math Test 1 – Solutions and Explanations

1) The correct answer is D. Because two negatives make a positive, we know that $-(-5) = 5$. So, we can substitute this into the equation in order to solve it: $-(-5) + 3 = 5 + 3 = 8$

2) The correct answer is D. For problems that ask you to find the largest possible product of two even integers, first you need to divide the sum by 2. The sum in this problem is 22, so divide by 2.
$22 \div 2 = 11$

Now take the result from this division and find the 2 nearest even integers that are 1 number higher and lower.
$11 + 1 = 12$
$11 - 1 = 10$

Then multiply these two numbers together in order to get the product.
$12 \times 10 = 120$

3) The correct answer is C. Multiply the numerators: $1 \times 2 = 2$. Then multiply the denominators: $3 \times 3 = 9$. These numbers form the new fraction: $^2/_9$

4) The correct answer is B. Remember to invert the second fraction by putting the denominator on the top and the numerator on the bottom. So the second fraction $\frac{4}{7}$ becomes $\frac{7}{4}$ when inverted. Use the inverted fraction to solve the problem: $\frac{1}{5} \div \frac{4}{7} = \frac{1}{5} \times \frac{7}{4} = \frac{7}{20}$

5) The correct answer is A.

STEP 1: To find the LCD, you have to look at the factors for each denominator. Factors are the numbers that equal a product when they are multiplied by each other. So, the factors of 9 are:
$1 \times 9 = 9$
$3 \times 3 = 9$

The factors of 27 are:
$1 \times 27 = 27$
$3 \times 9 = 27$

STEP 2: Determine which factors are common to both denominators by comparing the lists of factors. In this problem, the factors of 3 and 9 are common to the denominators of both fractions. We can illustrate the common factors as shown below. We saw that the factors of 9 were:
1 × **9** = 9
3 × 3 = 9

The factors of 27 were:
1 × 27 = 27
3 × **9** = 27

So, the numbers in bold above are the common factors.

STEP 3: Multiply the common factors to get the lowest common denominator. The numbers that are in bold above are then used to calculate the lowest common denominator: $3 \times 9 = 27$

STEP 4: Convert the denominator of each fraction to the LCD. You convert the fraction by referring to the factors from step 3. Multiply the numerator and the denominator by the same factor. We convert the first fraction as follows: $\frac{1}{9} \times \frac{3}{3} = \frac{3}{27}$

We do not need to convert the second fraction of $\frac{9}{27}$ because it already has the LCD.

STEP 5: When both fractions have the same denominator, you can perform the operation to solve the problem: $\frac{1}{9} + \frac{9}{27} = \frac{3}{27} + \frac{9}{27} = \frac{12}{27}$

6) The correct answer is D.

STEP 1: Look at the factors of the numerator and denominator. The factors of 12 are:
1 × 12 = 12
2 × 6 = 12
3 × 4 = 12

You will remember that the factors of 27 are:
1 × 27 = 27
3 × 9 = 27

So, we can see that the numerator and denominator have the common factor of 3.

STEP 2: Simplify the fraction by dividing the numerator and denominator by the common factor.
Simplify the numerator: 12 ÷ 3 = 4
Then simplify the denominator: 27 ÷ 3 = 9

STEP 3: Use the results from step 2 to form the new fraction. The numerator from step 2 is 4. The denominator is 9. So, the new fraction is $\frac{4}{9}$

7) The correct answer is C.

STEP 1: Convert the first mixed number to an integer plus a fraction.

$3\frac{1}{3} = 3 + \frac{1}{3}$

STEP 2: Then multiply the integer by a fraction whose numerator and denominator are the same as the denominator of the existing fraction.

$3 + \frac{1}{3} =$

$\left(3 \times \frac{3}{3}\right) + \frac{1}{3} =$

$\frac{9}{3} + \frac{1}{3}$

STEP 3: Add the two fractions to get your new fraction.

$\frac{9}{3} + \frac{1}{3} = \frac{10}{3}$

Then repeat the steps to convert the second mixed number to a fraction, using the same steps that we have just completed for the first mixed number.

$2\frac{1}{2} =$

$2 + \frac{1}{2} =$

$\left(2 \times \frac{2}{2}\right) + \frac{1}{2} =$

$\frac{4}{2} + \frac{1}{2} = \frac{5}{2}$

Now that you have converted both mixed numbers to fractions, find the lowest common denominator and subtract to solve.

$\frac{10}{3} - \frac{5}{2} =$

$\left(\frac{10}{3} \times \frac{2}{2}\right) - \left(\frac{5}{2} \times \frac{3}{3}\right) =$

$\frac{20}{6} - \frac{15}{6} =$

$\frac{5}{6}$

8) The correct answer is A. There are no parentheses or exponents in this problem, so we need to direct our attention to the multiplication and division first. When you see a problem like this one, you need to do the multiplication and division from left to right. This means that you take the number to the left of the multiplication or division symbol and multiply or divide that number on the left by the number on the right of the symbol. So, in our problem we need to multiply –6 by 3 and then divide 4 by 2.

You can see the order of operations more clearly if you put in parentheses to group the numbers together.

$-6 \times 3 - 4 \div 2 =$

$(-6 \times 3) - (4 \div 2) =$

$-18 - 2 = -20$

9) The correct answer is B.

For this type of problem, do the operations inside the **parentheses** first.

$\frac{5 \times (7-4)^2 + 3 \times 8}{5 - 6 \div (4-1)} =$

$\frac{5 \times (3)^2 + 3 \times 8}{5 - 6 \div 3}$

Then do the operation on the **exponent**.

$$\frac{5\times(3)^2+3\times8}{5-6\div3}=$$

$$\frac{5\times(3\times3)+3\times8}{5-6\div3}$$

$$\frac{5\times9+3\times8}{5-6\div3}$$

Then do the **multiplication** and **division**.

$$\frac{5\times9+3\times8}{5-6\div3}=$$

$$\frac{(5\times9)+(3\times8)}{5-(6\div3)}=$$

$$\frac{45+24}{5-2}$$

Then do the **addition** and **subtraction**.

$$\frac{45+24}{5-2}=\frac{69}{3}$$

In this case, we can then simplify the fraction since both the numerator and denominator are divisible by 3.

$$\frac{69}{3}=69\div3=23$$

10) The correct answer is B. To solve questions involving percentages, remember that there are three general ways to express percentages.

TYPE 1: Percentages as fractions
Percentages can always be expressed as the number over one hundred.
So 45% = $^{45}/_{100}$

TYPE 2: Percentages as simplified fractions
Percentages can also be expressed as simplified fractions. In order to simplify the fraction, you have to find the largest number that will go into both the numerator and denominator.
For 45%, the fraction is $^{45}/_{100}$, and the numerator and denominator are both divisible by 5.
To simplify the numerator: 45 ÷ 5 = 9.
To simplify the denominator: 100 ÷ 5 = 20.
This results in the simplified fraction of $^{9}/_{20}$.

TYPE 3: Percentages as decimals
Percentages can also be expressed as decimals.
45% = $^{45}/_{100}$ = 45 ÷ 100 = 0.45

In our problem, if $t\%$ subscribe to digital TV packages, then $100\% - t\%$ do not subscribe. In other words, since a percentage is any given number out of 100%, the percentage of students who do not subscribe is represented by this equation: $(100\% - t\%)$

This equation is then multiplied by the total number of students (n) in order to determine the number of students who do not subscribe to digital TV packages:
$(100\% - t\%) \times n$

11) The correct answer is C.

STEP 1: You can simplify the first fraction because both the numerator and denominator are divisible by 3: $^3/_6 \div {^3/_3} = {^1/_2}$

STEP 2: Then divide the denominator of the second fraction ($^x/_{14}$) by the denominator of the simplified fraction ($^1/_2$) from above: $14 \div 2 = 7$

STEP 3: Now, multiply the number from step 2 by the numerator of the fraction we calculated in step 1 in order to get your result: $1 \times 7 = 7$

You can check your answer as follows:
$^3/_6 = {^7/_{14}}$
$^3/_6 \div {^3/_3} = {^1/_2}$
$^7/_{14} \div {^7/_7} = {^1/_2}$

12) The correct answer is D. This problem is asking for the ratio of non-faulty mp3 players to the quantity of faulty mp3 players. Therefore, you must put the quantity of non-faulty mp3 players before the colon in the ratio. In this problem, 1% of the players are faulty.

$1\% \times 100 = 1$ faulty player in every 100 players
$100 - 1 = 99$ non-faulty players

So, the ratio is 99:1. As explained in the study tip after the question, the number before the colon and the number after the colon can be added together to get the total quantity.

13) The correct answer is B. The sales price of each cell phone is four times the cost. The cost is expressed as x, so the sales price is $4x$. The difference between the sales price of each cell phone and the cost of each cell phone is the profit. In this problem, the sales price is $4x$ and the cost is x.

Sales Price − Cost = Profit
$4x - x$ = Profit
$3x$ = Profit

14) The correct answer is D. The price of the internet connection is always 5 times the speed.

$10 = 2 \times 5$
$20 = 4 \times 5$
$30 = 6 \times 5$
$40 = 8 \times 5$

So, the price of the internet connection (represented by variable P) equals the speed (represented by variable s) times 5: $P = s \times 5$

15) The correct answer is C. To calculate the mean, add up all of the values: $1 + 2 + 3 + 4 + 5 + 5 + 8 + 8 + 9 = 45$. There are 9 numbers in the set, so we need to divide by 9: $45 \div 9 = 5$

16) The correct answer is C. To find the median, first you have to put the numbers in the data set in the correct order from lowest to highest: 3, 12, 18, **20**, 25, 28, 30. The median is the middle number in the set, which is 20 in this question.

17) The correct answer is D. For questions on absolute value, do the operation and then make the number inside the lines positive.

$|3-6| = |-3|$

$|-3| = 3$

18) The correct answer is C. Study the solution below, which highlights the order to carry out the FOIL method to perform the operations on the terms.

$(3x-2y)^2 = (3x-2y)(3x-2y)$

FIRST: The first terms in each set of parentheses are $3x$ and $3x$: $(\mathbf{3x} - 2y)(\mathbf{3x} - 2y)$

$3x \times 3x = 9x^2$

OUTSIDE: The terms on the outside are $3x$ and $-2y$: $(\mathbf{3x} - 2y)(3x \mathbf{- 2y})$

$3x \times -2y = -6xy$

INSIDE: The terms on the inside are $-2y$ and $3x$: $(3x \mathbf{- 2y})(\mathbf{3x} - 2y)$

$-2y \times 3x = -6xy$

LAST: The last terms in each set are $-2y$ and $-2y$: $(3x \mathbf{- 2y})(3x \mathbf{- 2y})$

$-2y \times -2y = 4y^2$

All of these individual results are put together for your final answer to the question.

$9x^2 - 6xy - 6xy + 4y^2 =$

$9x^2 - 12xy + 4y^2$

19) The correct answer is D. In order to solve this type of problem, you must do long division of the polynomial. Remember that you are subtracting the terms when you perform each part of the long division, so you need to be careful with negatives.

$$
\begin{array}{r}
x + 2 \\
x-3 \overline{) x^2 - x - 6} \\
\underline{x^2 - 3x} \\
2x - 6 \\
\underline{2x - 6} \\
0
\end{array}
$$

20) The correct answer is A.

$4x^2 + 2xy - y^2 =$

$(4 \times 2^2) + (2 \times 2 \times -2) - (-2^2) =$

$(4 \times 2 \times 2) + (2 \times 2 \times -2) - (-2 \times -2) =$

$(4 \times 4) + (2 \times -4) - (4) =$

$16 + (-8) - 4 =$

$16 - 12 = 4$

21) The correct answer is A.

STEP 1: Factor the equation.

$x^2 + 6x + 8 = 0$

$(x + 2)(x + 4) = 0$

STEP 2: Now substitute 0 for x in the first pair of parentheses.

$(0 + 2)(x + 4) = 0$

$2(x + 4) = 0$

$2x + 8 = 0$

$2x + 8 - 8 = 0 - 8$

$2x = -8$

$2x \div 2 = -8 \div 2$

$x = -4$

STEP 3: Then substitute 0 for x in the second pair of parentheses.

$(x + 2)(x + 4) = 0$

$(x + 2)(0 + 4) = 0$

$(x + 2)4 = 0$

$4x + 8 = 0$

$4x + 8 - 8 = 0 - 8$

$4x = -8$

$4x \div 4 = -8 \div 4$

$x = -2$

22) The correct answer is B. Remember that the line that divides the numerator and denominator in a fraction can be expressed as the division symbol.

$$\frac{\frac{1}{7}}{\frac{x}{3}} =$$

$$\frac{1}{7} \div \frac{x}{3}$$

To divide, invert the second fraction. To invert, you can swap the positions of the numerator and denominator.

$$\frac{1}{7} \div \frac{x}{3} =$$

$$\frac{1}{7} \times \frac{3}{x}$$

Then multiply to solve.

$$\frac{1}{7} \times \frac{3}{x} =$$

$$\frac{1 \times 3}{7 \times x} = \frac{3}{7x}$$

23) The correct answer is D. Eliminate the radical in the denominator by multiplying both sides of the equation by the radical.

$$\frac{30}{\sqrt{x^2 - 75}} = 6$$

$$\frac{30}{\sqrt{x^2 - 75}} \times \sqrt{x^2 - 75} = 6 \times \sqrt{x^2 - 75}$$

$$30 = 6\sqrt{x^2 - 75}$$

Then eliminate the integer in front of the radical.

$$30 = 6\sqrt{x^2 - 75}$$

$$30 \div 6 = \left(6\sqrt{x^2 - 75}\right) \div 6$$

$$5 = \sqrt{x^2 - 75}$$

Then eliminate the radical by squaring both sides of the equation, and solve for *x*.

$$5 = \sqrt{x^2 - 75}$$

$$5^2 = \left(\sqrt{x^2 - 75}\right)^2$$

$$25 = x^2 - 75$$

$$25 + 75 = x^2 - 75 + 75$$

$$100 = x^2$$

$$x = 10$$

24) The correct answer is D. Find the lowest common denominator. Since *x* is common to both denominators, we can convert the denominator of the second fraction to the LCD by multiplying by $(x - 6)$.

$$\frac{x^5}{x^2 - 6x} + \frac{5}{x} =$$

$$\frac{x^5}{x^2 - 6x} + \left(\frac{5}{x} \times \frac{x - 6}{x - 6}\right) =$$

$$\frac{x^5}{x^2 - 6x} + \frac{5x - 30}{x^2 - 6x} =$$

$$\frac{x^5 + 5x - 30}{x^2 - 6x}$$

25) The correct answer is A. The base number in this example is 11. So, we add the exponents: 5 + 3 = 8 for the exponent. So, $11^5 \times 11^3 = 11^{(5+3)} = 11^8$

26) The correct answer is C. When the base numbers are the same and you need to multiply the base numbers, you add the exponents. $x^4 \times x^2 = x^6$ ($x^6 = x \times x \times x \times x \times x \times x$)

27) The correct answer is B. The base number in this example is 10. So, we subtract the exponents: 6 − 4 = 2 for the exponent. So, $10^6 \div 10^4 = 10^{(6-4)} = 10^2$

28) The correct answer is D. For inequality problems like this, look to see if both the equation and inequality have any variables or terms in common. In this problem, both contain $x - 2$. The cost of one movie ticket is represented by y, and y is equal to $x - 2$. Therefore, we can substitute values as shown below.

$x - 2 > 5$
$y > 5$

If two tickets are being purchased, we need to solve for $2y$.
$y \times 2 > 5 \times 2$
$2y > 10$

29) The correct answer is A. Multiply the numerator of the first fraction by the numerator of the second fraction. Then multiply the denominators.

$$\frac{2x^3}{5} \times \frac{4}{x^2} = \frac{8x^3}{5x^2}$$

Then factor the numerator and denominator.

$$\frac{8x^3}{5x^2} = \frac{8x(x^2)}{5(x^2)}$$

Then we can cancel out x^2 to solve the problem.

$$\frac{8x(x^2)}{5(x^2)} = \frac{8x}{5}$$

30) The correct answer is A. The first step in solving the problem is to invert and multiply by the second fraction.

$$\frac{6x+6}{x^2} \div \frac{3x+3}{x^3} =$$

$$\frac{6x+6}{x^2} \times \frac{x^3}{3x+3} =$$

$$\frac{x^3(6x+6)}{x^2(3x+3)}$$

Then factor the numerator and denominator. $(x + 1)$ is common to both the numerator and the denominator, so we can factor that out.

$$\frac{x^3(6x+6)}{x^2(3x+3)} =$$

$$\frac{x^3 6(x+1)}{x^2 3(x+1)}$$

Now cancel out the $(x + 1)$.

$$\frac{x^3 6(x+1)}{x^2 3(x+1)} =$$

$$\frac{x^3 6}{x^2 3} =$$

$$\frac{6x^3}{3x^2}$$

Now factor out x^2 and cancel it out.

$$\frac{6x^3}{3x^2} =$$

$$\frac{6x \times x^2}{3x^2} =$$

$$\frac{6x}{3}$$

The numerator and denominator share the factor of 3, so cancel out further in order to get your final result.

$$\frac{6x}{3} = \frac{3 \times 2 \times x}{3} = 2x$$

31) The correct answer is A. Remember that any real number squared will always equal a positive number. Since 8 is added to the first value x^2, the result will always be 8 or greater. In other words, since x^2 is always a positive number, the result of the equation would never be 0. So, there are zero solutions for this equation.

32) The correct answer is C. Since 9 is subtracted from x^2, x^2 needs to be equal to 9. Both 3 and −3 solve the equation. So, there are two solutions for this equation.

33) The correct answer is C. For some basic equation problems, you will see two equations which have the same two variables, like *J* and *T* in the problem above. In order to solve the problem, take the second equation and isolate *J* on one side of the equation. By doing this, you define variable *J* in terms of variable *T*.

$J + 2T = \$40$

$J + 2T - 2T = \$40 - 2T$

$J = \$40 - 2T$

Now substitute \$40 − $2T$ for variable J in the first equation to solve for variable T.
$2J + T = 50$
$2(40 - 2T) + T = 50$
$80 - 4T + T = 50$
$80 - 3T = 50$
$80 - 3T + 3T = 50 + 3T$
$80 = 50 + 3T$
$80 - 50 = 50 - 50 + 3T$
$30 = 3T$
$30 \div 3 = 3T \div 3$
$10 = T$

So, now that we know that a T-shirt costs \$10, we can substitute this value in one of the equations in order to find the value for the jeans, which is variable J.
$2J + T = 50$
$2J + 10 = 50$
$2J + 10 - 10 = 50 - 10$
$2J = 40$
$2J \div 2 = 40 \div 2$
$J = 20$

Now solve for Sarah's purchase. If she purchased one pair of jeans and one T-shirt, then she paid: \$10 + \$20 = \$30

34) The correct answer is C. Look at the x term of the second equation, which is $2x$. In order to eliminate the x variable, we need to multiply the first equation by 2 and then subtract the second equation from this result.

$x + 4y = 30$
$(2 \times x) + (2 \times 4y) = (30 \times 2)$
$2x + 8y = 60$

Now subtract the two equations.

$$\begin{array}{r} 2x + 8y = 60 \\ -(2x + 2y = 36) \\ \hline 6y = 24 \end{array}$$

Then solve for y.
$6y = 24$
$6y \div 6 = 24 \div 6$
$y = 4$

Using our first equation $x + 4y = 30$, substitute the value of 4 for y to solve for x.
$x + 4y = 30$
$x + (4 \times 4) = 30$
$x + 16 = 30$

$$x+16-16=30-16$$
$$x=14$$

35) The correct answer is B.

To solve this type of problem, do multiplication on the items in parentheses first.
$3x - 2(x + 5) = -8$
$3x - 2x - 10 = -8$

Then deal with the integers by putting them on one side of the equation.
$3x - 2x - 10 + 10 = -8 + 10$
$3x - 2x = 2$

Then solve for x.
$3x - 2x = 2$
$1x = 2$
$x = 2$

36) The correct answer is B. For questions on systems of equations like this one, you should look at the multiplication equation first. Ask yourself, what are the factors of 20? We know that 20 is the product of the following:

$1 \times 20 = 20$
$2 \times 10 = 20$
$4 \times 5 = 20$

Now add each of the two factors together to solve the first equation.
$1 + 20 = 21$
$2 + 10 = 12$
$4 + 5 = 9$

(4, 5) solves both equations, so it is the correct answer.

37) The correct answer is D. For square root problems like this one, you need to remember certain mathematical principles. First, remember to factor the number inside the square root sign. The factors of 45 are:
$1 \times 45 = 45$
$3 \times 15 = 45$
$5 \times 9 = 45$

Then look to see if any of these factors have square roots that are whole numbers. In this case, the only factor whose square root is a whole number is 9. Now find the square root of 9.
$\sqrt{9} = 3$

Finally, you need to put this number at the front of the square root sign and put the other factor inside the square root sign in order to solve the problem.
$$\sqrt{45} = \sqrt{9 \times 5} = \sqrt{3 \times 3 \times 5} = 3\sqrt{5}$$

38) The correct answer is D. First you need to find perfect squares for the factors of the amounts inside the radical signs. 16, 36, and 9 are perfect squares because $16 = 4^2$, $36 = 6^2$, and $9 = 3^2$.

$\sqrt{32} + 2\sqrt{72} + 3\sqrt{18} =$

$\sqrt{2 \times 16} + 2\sqrt{2 \times 36} + 3\sqrt{2 \times 9}$

Then expand the amounts inside the radicals for the factors and simplify.

$\sqrt{2 \times 16} + 2\sqrt{2 \times 36} + 3\sqrt{2 \times 9} =$

$\sqrt{2 \times (4 \times 4)} + 2\sqrt{2 \times (6 \times 6)} + 3\sqrt{2 \times (3 \times 3)} =$

$4\sqrt{2} + (2 \times 6)\sqrt{2} + (3 \times 3)\sqrt{2} =$

$4\sqrt{2} + 12\sqrt{2} + 9\sqrt{2} =$

$25\sqrt{2}$

39) The correct answer is A. Multiply the numbers inside the square root signs first: $6 \times 5 = 30$.

Then put this result inside a square root symbol for your answer: $\sqrt{30}$

40) The correct answer is B. In this problem, you have to find the cube roots of the numerator and denominator in order to eliminate the radical. Remember that the cube root is the number which satisfies the equation when multiplied by itself two times.

$$\sqrt[3]{\frac{64}{125}} = \sqrt[3]{\frac{4 \times 4 \times 4}{5 \times 5 \times 5}} = 4/5$$

41) The correct answer is C. The sum of all three angles inside a triangle is always 180 degrees. So, we need to deduct the degrees given from 180° to find out the total degrees of the two other angles: 180° − 36° = 144°

Now divide this result by two in order to determine the degrees for each angle: 144° ÷ 2 = 72°

42) The correct answer is D. The area of a rectangle is equal to its length times its width. This football field is 30 yards wide and 100 yards long, so now we can substitute the values.
rectangle area = width × length
rectangle area = 30 × 100
rectangle area = 3000

43) The correct answer is D. Substitute the values into the formula in order to find the solution for this problem:

$\sqrt{A^2 + B^2} = C$

$\sqrt{5^2 + 12^2} = C$

$\sqrt{25 + 144} = C$

$\sqrt{169} = C$

13 cm = C

44) The correct answer is C. The base length of the triangle described in the problem, which is line segment YZ, is not given. So, we need to calculate the base length using the Pythagorean Theorem. According to the Pythagorean Theorem, the length of the hypotenuse is equal to the square root of the sum of the squares of the two other sides.

$\sqrt{4^2 + base^2} = 5$

$\sqrt{16 + base^2} = 5$

Now square each side of the equation in order to solve for the base length.

$\sqrt{16 + base^2} = 5$

$(\sqrt{16 + base^2})^2 = 5^2$

$16 + base^2 = 25$

$16 - 16 + base^2 = 25 - 16$

$base^2 = 9$

$\sqrt{base^2} = \sqrt{9}$

$base = 3$

Now solve for the area of the triangle.
triangle area = (base × height) ÷ 2
triangle area = (3 × 4) ÷ 2
triangle area = 12 ÷ 2
triangle area = 6

45) The correct answer is B.

Write out the formula.
(length × 2) + (width × 2)

Then substitute the values.
(5 × 2) + (3 × 2)
10 + 6 = 16

46) The correct answer is B. Substitute the value of the diameter into the formula to calculate the circumference.
circumference = diameter × π
circumference = 12π

47) The correct answer is D. To calculate the volume of a box, you need the formula for a rectangular solid: volume = base × width × height

Now substitute the values from the problem into the formula.
volume = 20 × 15 × 25
volume = 7500

48) The correct answer is B. First, find the midpoint of the x coordinates for (**−4**, 2) and (**2**,−4).
midpoint $x = (x_1 + x_2) \div 2$
midpoint $x = (-4 + 2) \div 2$
midpoint $x = -2 \div 2$
midpoint $x = -1$

Then find the midpoint of the y coordinates for (−4, **2**) and (2,**−4**).
midpoint $y = (y_1 + y_2) \div 2$
midpoint $y = (2 + -4) \div 2$
midpoint $y = -2 \div 2$

midpoint $y = -1$
So, the midpoint is $(-1, -1)$

49) The correct answer is C. The problem states the y intercept, so use the slope-intercept formula to solve.
$y = mx + b$
$165 = m5 + 15$
$165 - 15 = m5 + 15 - 15$
$150 = m5$
$150 \div 5 = m5 \div 5$
$30 = m$

50) The correct answer is A. Find the solutions for the x and y intercepts separately as shown below. First, substitute 0 for y in order to find the *x* intercept.

$x^2 + 4y^2 = 64$
$x^2 + (4 \times 0) = 64$
$x^2 + 0 = 64$
$x^2 = 64$
$x = 8$

Then substitute 0 for x in order to find the *y* intercept.
$x^2 + 4y^2 = 64$
$(0 \times 0) + 4y^2 = 64$
$0 + 4y^2 = 64$
$4y^2 \div 4 = 64 \div 4$
$y^2 = 16$
$y = 4$
So, the *x* intercept is (8, 0) and the *y* intercept is (0, 4).

TABE Practice Math Test 2 with Study Tips

Number and data problems:

1) Which of the following shows the numbers ordered from least to greatest?
A) $-\frac{1}{4}$, $\frac{1}{8}$, $\frac{1}{6}$, 1
B) $-\frac{1}{4}$, $\frac{1}{8}$, 1, $\frac{1}{6}$
C) $-\frac{1}{4}$, $\frac{1}{6}$, $\frac{1}{8}$, 1
D) $-\frac{1}{4}$, 1, $\frac{1}{8}$, $\frac{1}{6}$

> In order to answer questions on ordering fractions and other numbers from least to greatest or greatest to least, remember these principles: (a) Negative numbers are less than positive numbers; (b) When two fractions have the same numerator, the fraction with the smaller number in the denominator is the larger fraction.

2) The numbers in the following list are ordered from greatest to least: θ, η, $\frac{25}{13}$, $\frac{10}{9}$, $\frac{1}{3}$
Which of the following could be the value of η?
A) $\sqrt{36}$
B) $\frac{25}{14}$
C) $\frac{24}{13}$
D) 1.91

> This problem is asking you to determine missing values from an ordered list of fractions and other numbers. You may find it easier to solve problems like this one if you convert the fractions to decimals.

3) If $7x$ is between 5 and 6, which of the following could be the value of x?
A) $\frac{2}{3}$
B) $\frac{3}{4}$
C) $\frac{5}{8}$
D) $\frac{7}{8}$

> To solve the problem, set up an inequality as follows: $5 < 7x < 6$. Then put the fractions from the answer choices in for x in order to solve the problem. When a problem asks you to multiply a whole number by a fraction, multiply the whole number by the numerator and then divide this result by the denominator.

4) The temperature on Saturday was 62° F at 5:00 PM and 38° F at 11:00 PM. If the temperature fell at a constant rate on Saturday, what was the temperature at 9:00 PM?
A) 58° F
B) 54° F
C) 50° F
D) 46° F

> This question assesses your knowledge of performing operations on integers. Here, we have to perform the operations of subtraction, multiplication, and division.

5) The Smith family is having lunch in a diner. They buy hot dogs and hamburgers to eat. The hot dogs cost $2.50 each, and the hamburgers cost $4 each. They buy 3 hamburgers. They also buy hot dogs. The total value of their purchase is $22. How many hot dogs did they buy?

A) 2
B) 3
C) 4
D) 5

> This question assesses your knowledge of performing addition, subtraction, multiplication, and division on integers in a single practical problem. Set up an equation, with the number of hot dogs represented by *D* and the number of hamburgers represented by *H*.

6) A painter needs to paint 8 rooms, each of which have a surface area of 2000 square feet. If one bucket of paint covers 900 square feet, what is the fewest number of buckets of paint that must be used to complete all 8 rooms?

A) 3
B) 17
C) 18
D) 19

> This is a question that requires you to find the fewest multiples of an item. Be mindful of the words "fewest" and "greatest" in problems like this one, since it will normally be impossible to purchase a fractional part of the item in the question. Therefore, you will need to round your result up or down to the nearest whole number accordingly.

7) Soon Li jogged 3.6 miles in $^3/_4$ of an hour. What was her average jogging speed in miles per hour?

A) 5.0
B) 4.8
C) 4.2
D) 2.7

> This problem involves the calculation of miles per hour with fractional parts of hours. To solve the problem, divide the distance traveled by the time in order to get the speed in miles per hour.

8) How many 2 letter combinations can be made from the letter set: A E I O U?

A) 5
B) 10
C) 40
D) 120

> For combinations of *S* at a time from a set containing *N* items, use the formula: $(N!) \div [(N - S)! \times S!]$ For the question above, $N = 5$ and $S = 2$.

9) How many 4 letter permutations can be made from the letter set: A C K W Y?

A) 120
B) 100
C) 60
D) 9

Permutations are like combinations, except permutations take into account the order of the items in each group. For permutations of S at a time from a set containing N items, use the formula: $N! \div (N - S)!$ For the question above, $N = 5$ and $S = 4$.

10) Members of a weight loss group report their individual weight loss to the group leader every week. During the week, the following amounts in pounds were reported: 1, 1, 3, 2, 4, 3, 1, 2, and 1. What is the mode of the weight loss for the group?

A) 1 pound
B) 2 pounds
C) 3 pounds
D) 4 pounds

This is a question on mode. Mode is the value that occurs most frequently in a data set. For example, if 10 students scored 85 on a test, 6 students scored 90, and 4 students scored 80, the mode score is 85.

11) A student receives the following scores on her assignments during the term: 98.5, 85.5, 80.0, 97, 93, 92.5, 93, 87, 88, 82. What is the range of her scores?

A) 17.0
B) 18.0
C) 18.5
D) 89.65

This is a question on calculating range. To calculate range, the lowest value in the data set is deducted from the highest value in the data set.

12) Which of the following number lines represents seven values in which the median of the values exceeds the mean of the values?

A)

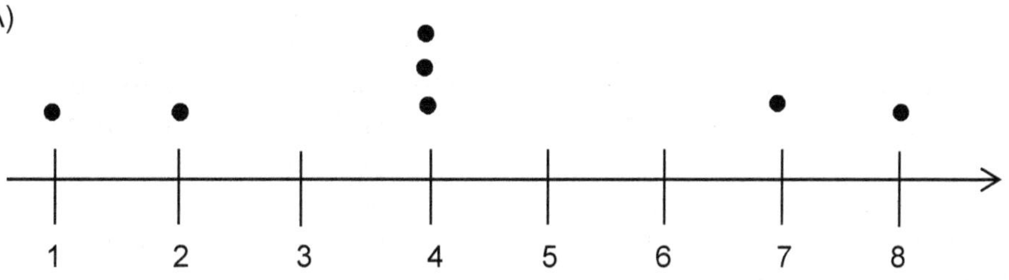

B)

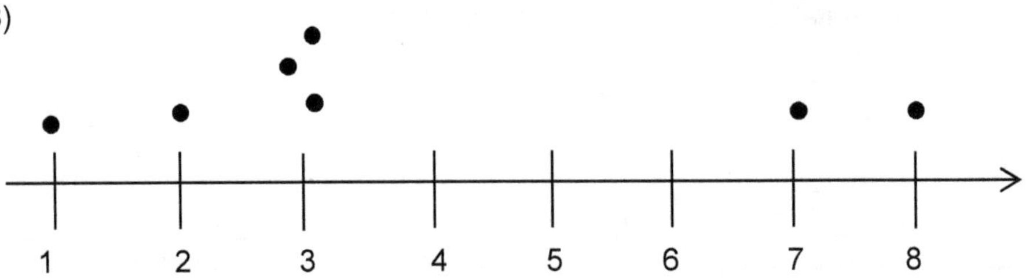

C)

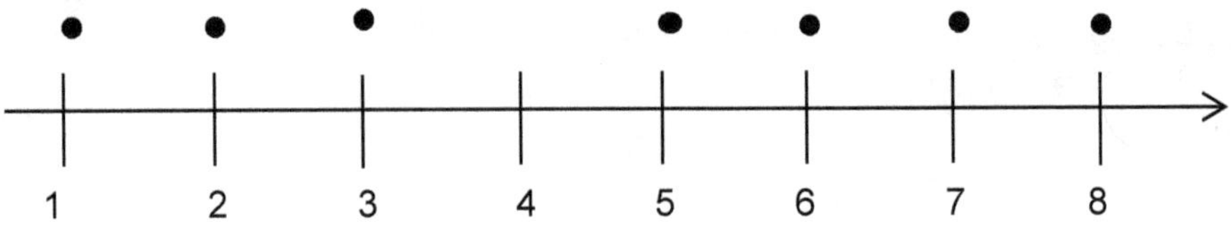

D)

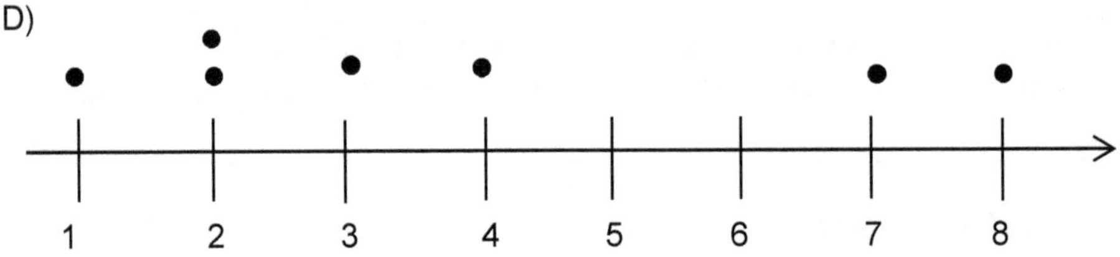

This is a question on reading number lines to determine the mean and median. You should first look to see how many dots there are above the lines. Then add up the individual values from each line to calculate the mean of each of the answer options. You can determine the median visually by seeing which number is midway on each of the lines.

13) A bag contains 5 red balloons, 10 orange balloons, 8 green balloons, and 12 purple balloons. If a balloon is drawn from the bag at random, what is the probability that it will be orange?

A) $\frac{2}{7}$ B) $\frac{1}{4}$ C) $\frac{1}{10}$ D) $\frac{1}{35}$

This is a question on calculating basic probability. First of all, calculate how many items there are in total in the data set, which is also called the "sample space" or (*S*). Then reduce the data set if further items are removed. Probability can be expressed as a fraction. The number of items available in the total data set at the time of the draw goes in the denominator. The chance of the desired outcome, which is also referred to as the event or (*E*), goes in the numerator of the fraction. You can determine the chance of the event by calculating how many items are available in the subset of the desired outcome.

14) The graph below shows the relationship between the total number of chicken sandwiches a restaurant sells and the total sales in dollars for the chicken sandwiches. What is the sales price per chicken sandwich?

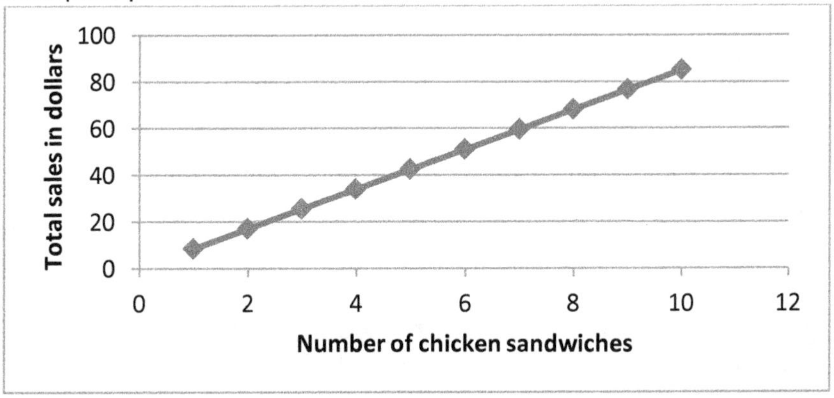

A) $4.00
B) $8.00
C) $8.50
D) $9.50

This is an example of a question that asks you to interpret a line graph in order to determine the price per unit of an item. To solve the problem, look at the graph and then divide the total sales in dollars by the total quantity sold in order to get the price per unit.

15) Mr. Rodriguez teaches a class of 25 students. Ten of the students in his class participate in drama club. In which graph below does the dark gray area represent the percentage of students who participate in drama club?

A)

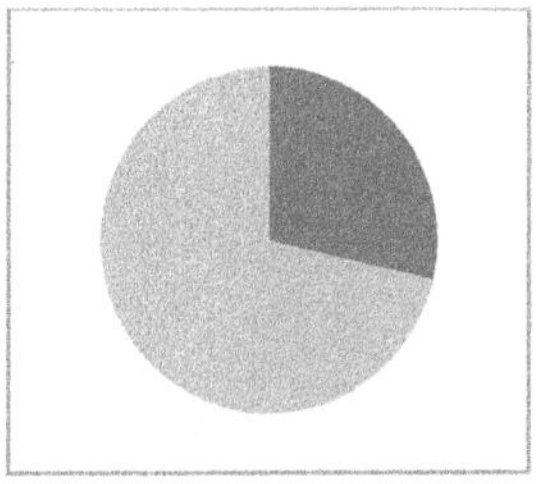

B)

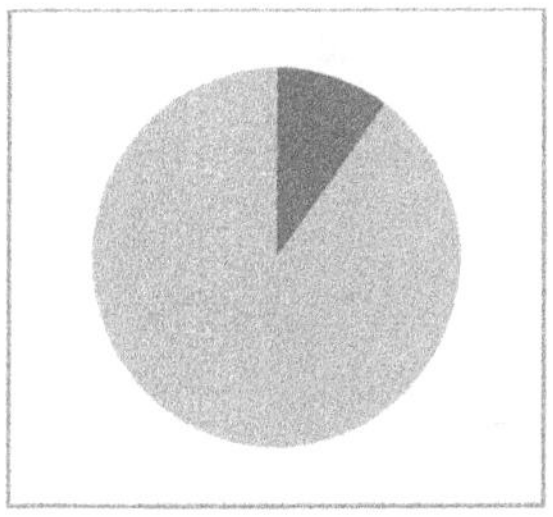

C)

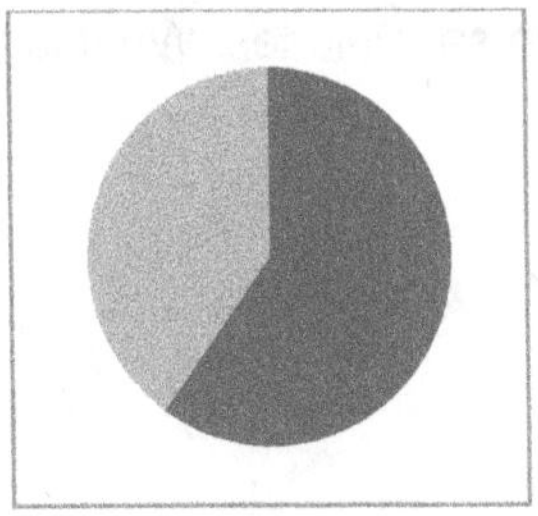

D)

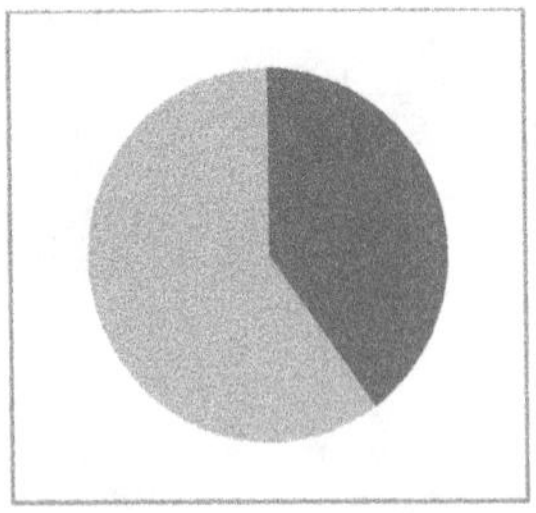

Questions like this one are asking you about how to express percentages using pie charts. Facts such as x students from y total students participate in a group can be represented as $^{x}/_{y}$.

16) In Brown County Elementary School, parents are advised to have their children vaccinated against five childhood diseases. According to the chart below, how many children were vaccinated against at least three diseases?

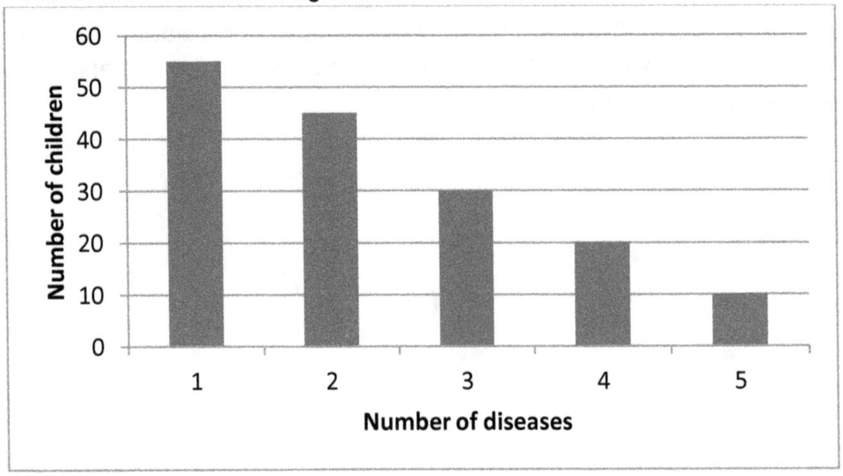

A) 30
B) 50
C) 60
D) 100

For data questions that ask you to interpret bar graphs or histograms, you need to read the problem carefully to determine what is represented on the horizontal axis (bottom) and the vertical axis (left side) of the graph. Histograms are like bar graphs, except they represent groups of data. We will look at histograms in the next practice test.

17) Express the following number in scientific notation: 19,875.246

A) 1.9875246×10^3
B) 1.9875246×10^4
C) 1.9875246×10^5
D) 1.9875246×10^6

This is a practice question on scientific notation. In scientific notation, you need to remember to multiply by a power of 10.

For example, the number 635,000 is written in scientific notation as 6.35×10^5.

The first step is to move the decimal point to the left, and then count the number of places to the right. The amount of decimal places that you move is the same number that you use for your exponent.

18) A zoo has reptiles, birds, quadrupeds, and fish. At the start of the year, they have a total of 1,500 creatures living in the zoo. The pie chart below shows percentages by category for the 1,500 creatures at the start of the year.

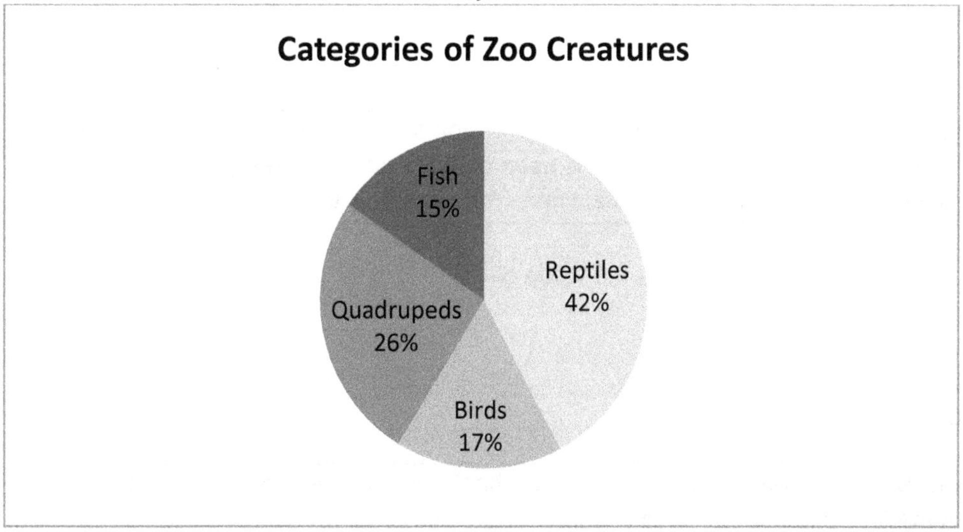

At the end of the year, the zoo still has 1,500 creatures, but reptiles constitute 40%, birds 23%, and quadrupeds 21%. How many more fish were there at the end of the year than at the beginning of the year?

A) 10
B) 11
C) 15
D) 16

This question is asking you to interpret a pie chart that shows percentages by category. If you are asked to calculate changes to the data in the categories in the chart, be sure to multiply by the percentages at the beginning of the year and then do a separate calculation using the percentages at the end of the year.

Algebra concepts and formulas:

19) If $\frac{3}{4}x - 2 = 4, x = ?$

A) $\frac{8}{3}$

B) $\frac{1}{8}$

C) 8

D) –8

This is a problem requiring you to solve an equation that contains a single variable, a fraction, and integers. First, isolate the integers and then eliminate the fraction. Finally, divide to find the value of the variable.

20) If $2(3x - 1) = 4(x + 1) - 3$, what is the value of x?

A) $x = {}^{3}/_{2}$

B) $x = {}^{2}/_{3}$

C) $x = {}^{4}/_{3}$

D) $x = {}^{3}/_{4}$

This problem requires you to solve an algebraic expression that contains one variable (x) on both sides of the equation. When the variable is used on both sides of the equation, you should perform the multiplication on the parentheticals first. Then isolate x to solve the problem.

21) If $x + y = 5$ and $a + b = 4$, what is the value of $(3x + 3y)(5a + 5b)$?

A) 9

B) 35

C) 200

D) 300

This problem involves expressions that contain more than one variable. First of all, factor each parenthetical in the final expression. Then substitute values in order to solve the problem.

22) Consider the inequality: $-3x + 14 < 5$

Which of the following values of x is a possible solution to the inequality above?

A) –3.1

B) 2.25

C) 2.65

D) 4.35

This question is assessing your understanding of inequalities. When dealing with inequalities, we first need to place the integers on one side of the inequality. Then deal with any negative numbers. Remember that when you divide or multiply by a negative number in inequality problems, you need to reverse the way that the inequality sign points.

23) $20 - \frac{3x}{4} \geq 17$, then $x \leq$?

A) –12

B) –4

C) 4

D) 0

This is another advanced question on inequalities. Deal with the fraction by multiplying both sides of the equation by the denominator. Then perform the other operations in order to solve the problem.

24) Which of the following equations is equivalent to $\frac{x}{5} + \frac{y}{2}$?

A) $\frac{x+y}{7}$

B) $\frac{2x+5y}{10}$

C) $\frac{5x+2y}{10}$

D) $\frac{2x+5y}{7}$

This problem is asking you to find an equivalent expression for a mathematical expression that contains fractions. To add fractions, find the lowest common denominator first and then add the numerators.

25) If $W = \frac{XY}{Z}$, then Z = ?

A) $\frac{XY}{W}$

B) $\frac{W}{XY}$

C) $\frac{1}{XY}$

D) $\frac{1}{WXY}$

To find this equivalent expression, isolate the variable that the question is asking for, performing multiplication and division as necessary.

26) Shanika works as a car salesperson. She earns $1,000 a month, plus $390 for each car she sells. If she wants to earn at least $4,000 this month, what is the minimum number of cars that she must sell this month?

A) 6
B) 7
C) 8
D) 9

This question requires using algebra to solve a practical problem. For problems like this one, read the facts carefully and set up an equation to find the missing variable or quantity.

27) $x^{4/9} = ?$

A) $\frac{4x}{9}$

B) $(\sqrt[9]{x})^4$

C) $(\sqrt[9]{x})^5$

D) $(\sqrt[5]{x})^9$

Place the base number inside the radical sign. The denominator of the exponent is the nth root of the radical. The numerator is new exponent. Example: $x^{3/7} = (\sqrt[7]{x})^3$

28) Toby is going to buy a car. The total purchase price of the car is represented by variable C. He will pay D dollars immediately, and then he will make equal payments (P) each month for a certain number of months (M). Which equation below represents the amount of his monthly payment (P)?

A) $\frac{C-D}{M}$

B) $\frac{C}{M} - D$

C) $\frac{M}{C-D}$

D) $D - \frac{C}{M}$

This problem requires you to set up an algebraic equation based on facts in a practical problem. In this problem, we need to calculate a monthly payment after a down payment has been made. Deduct the down payment from the purchase price, and then divide by the number of months to solve the problem.

29) Fatima drove into town at a rate of 50 miles per hour. She shopped in town for 20 minutes, and then drove home on the same route at a rate of 60 miles per hour. Which of the following equations best expresses the total time (Tt) that it took Fatima to make the journey and do the shopping? Note that the variable D represents the distance in miles from Fatima's house to town.

A) $Tt + 20 \text{ minutes} = 110 \times D$
B) $Tt + 20 \text{ minutes} = [(50 + 60) \div 2] \times D$
C) $Tt = [(D \div 50) + (D \div 60)] + 20 \text{ minutes}$
D) $Tt = D \div 110$

This problem asks you to set up an algebraic equation based on facts in a practical problem. In this problem, we need to calculate the time spent on a journey. Remember that time can be calculated by dividing the distance by the miles per hour.

30) A baseball team sells T-shirts and sweatpants to the public for a fundraising event. The total amount of money the team earned from these sales was $850. Variable *t* represents the number of T-shirts sold and variable *s* represents the number of sweatpants sold. The total sales in dollars is represented by the equation 25*t* + 30*s*. The amount earned by selling sweatpants is what fraction of the total amount earned?

A) *s*/850
B) 30*s*/850
C) (25*t* + 30*s*)/850
D) *t*/850

This practical problem asks you to express part of an algebraic equation as a fraction of the entire equation. You can sometimes substitute a numerical or dollar value for the entire expression, as in this problem.

31) Perform the operation: $10ab^5(5ab^7 - 4b^3 - 10a)$

A) $50a^2b^{12} + 40ab^8 - 100a^2b^5$
B) $50a^2b^{12} - 40ab^8 + 100a^2b^5$
C) $50a^2b^{12} + 40ab^8 + 100a^2b^5$
D) $50a^2b^{12} - 40ab^8 - 100a^2b^5$

For advanced problems on polynomials, remember to use the distributive property of multiplication. Remember to add the exponents on the terms that you multiply together.

32) $\dfrac{x^2 + 10x + 16}{x^2 + 11x + 18} \times \dfrac{x^2 + 9x}{x^2 + 17x + 72} = ?$

A) $\dfrac{9}{x+9}$

B) $\dfrac{x}{x+9}$

C) $\frac{x^2}{x^2+17x}$

D) $\frac{x+1}{x+8}$

For this type of advanced factoring problem, first you need to find the factors of the numerators and denominators of each fraction. When there are only addition signs in a quadratic expression, the factors will be binomials in the following format: (+)(+)

33) $\frac{5z-5}{z} \div \frac{6z-6}{5z^2} = ?$

A)

$\frac{6}{25z}$

B)

$\frac{30z^2+30}{5z^3}$

C)

$\frac{6z^2-6z}{25z^2-25z}$

D)

$\frac{25z}{6}$

When dividing fractions, you need to invert the second fraction and then multiply the two fractions together. Then look at the resulting numerator and denominator to see if you can factor and simplify.

34) 2 inches on a scale drawing represents *F* feet. Which of the following equations represents *F* + 1 feet on the drawing?

A) $\frac{2(F+1)}{F}$

B) $\frac{(F+1)}{F}$

C) $\frac{2}{F+1}$

D) $\frac{2F}{F+1}$

This question requires you to set up systems of equations for a scale drawing. Set up ratios for each of the measurements, and then cross multiply to solve.

Geometry and graphing – problems and formulas:

35) The graph of $y = 8 \div (x - 4)$ is shown below.

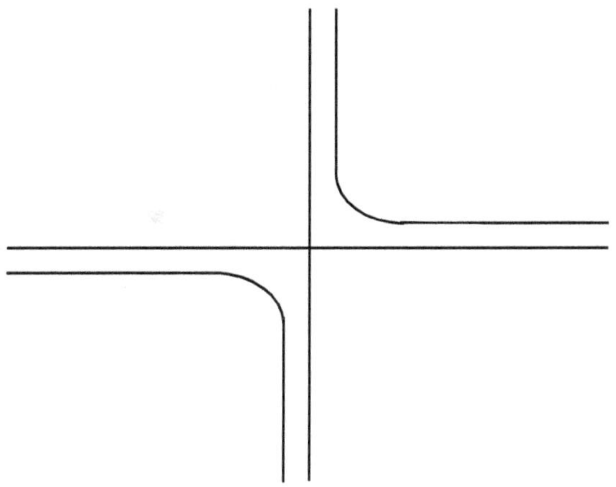

Which of the following is the best representation of $8 \div |(x - 4)|$?

A)

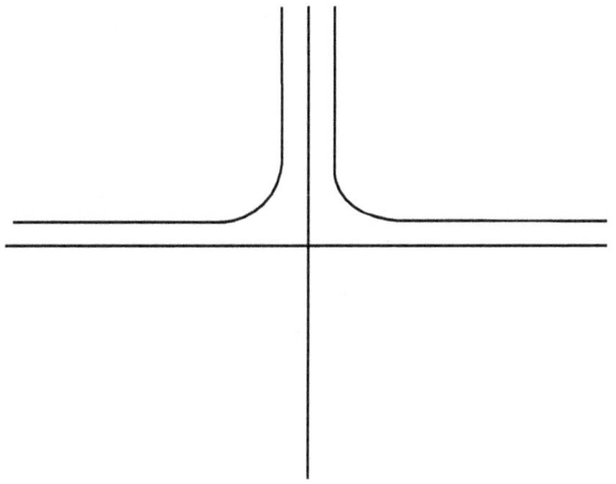

B)

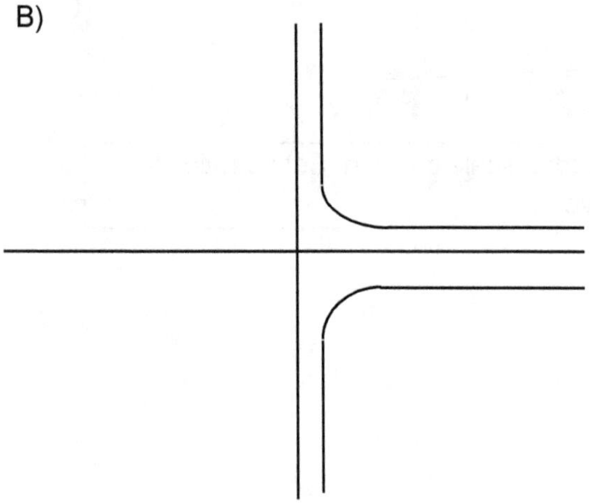

C)

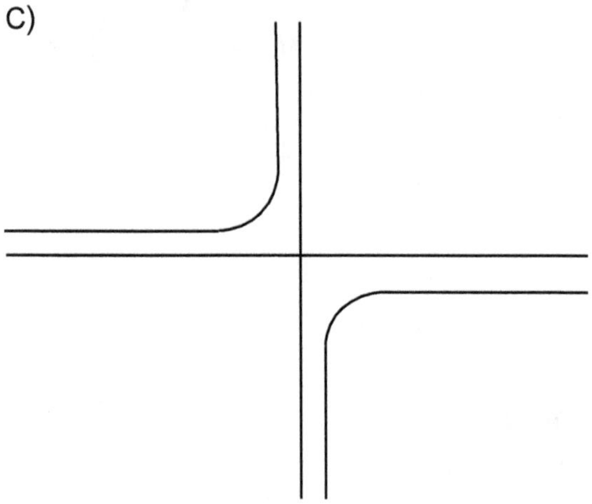

D)

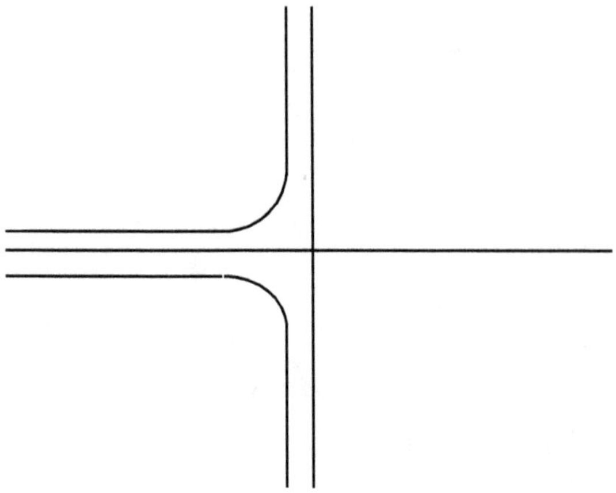

36) Which of the following shows the solution set of $-3x > 6$?

A)

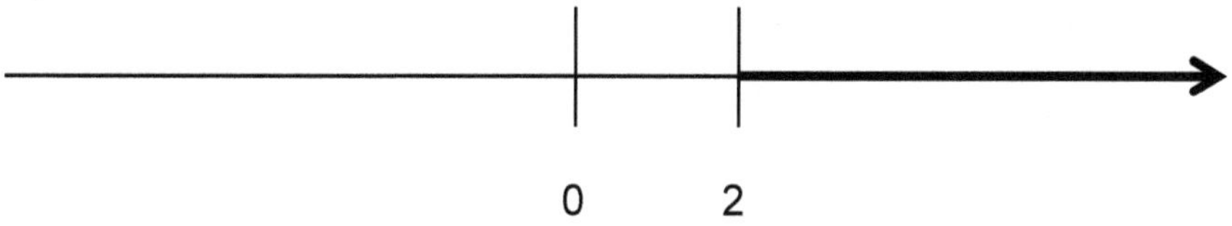

B)

C)

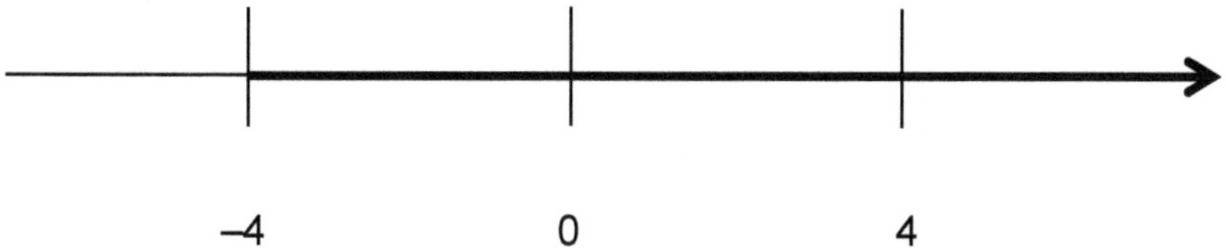

D)

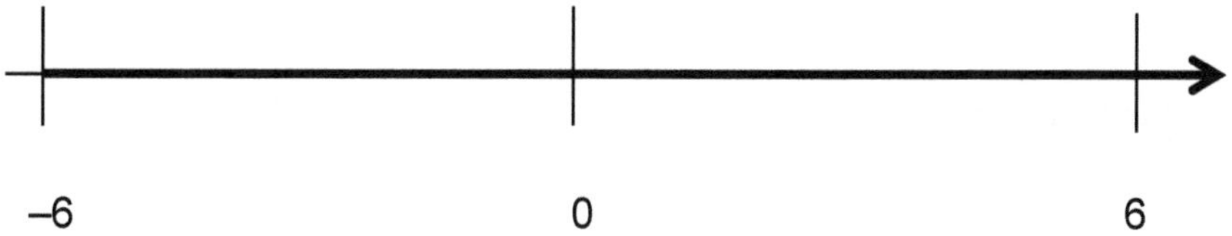

37) A mother has noticed that the more sugar her child eats, the more her child sleeps at night. Which of the following graphs best illustrates the relationship between the amount of sugar the child consumes and the child's amount of sleep?

A)

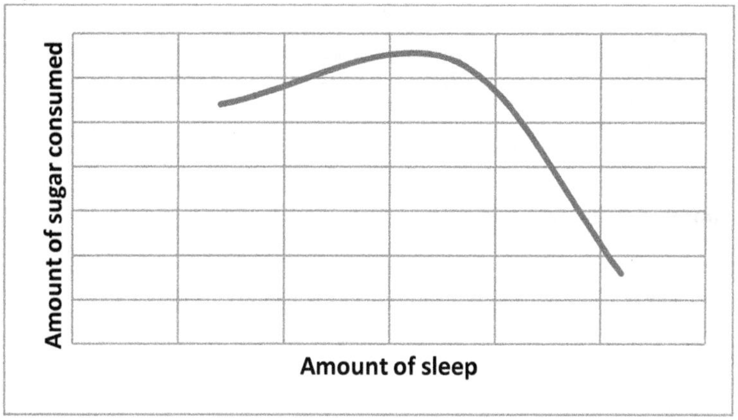

B)

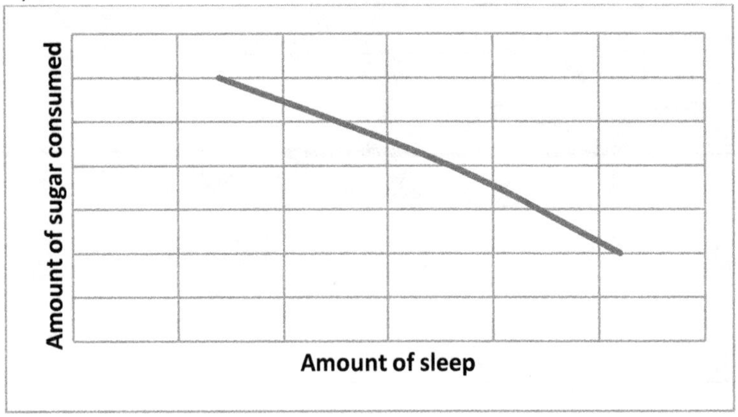
Amount of sugar consumed
Amount of sleep

C)

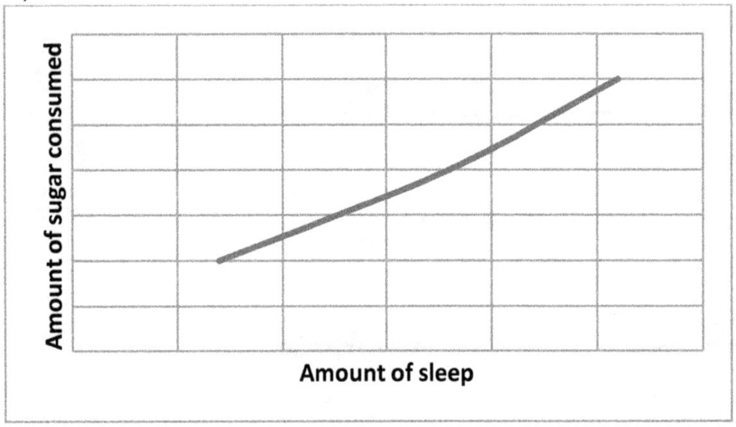
Amount of sugar consumed
Amount of sleep

D)

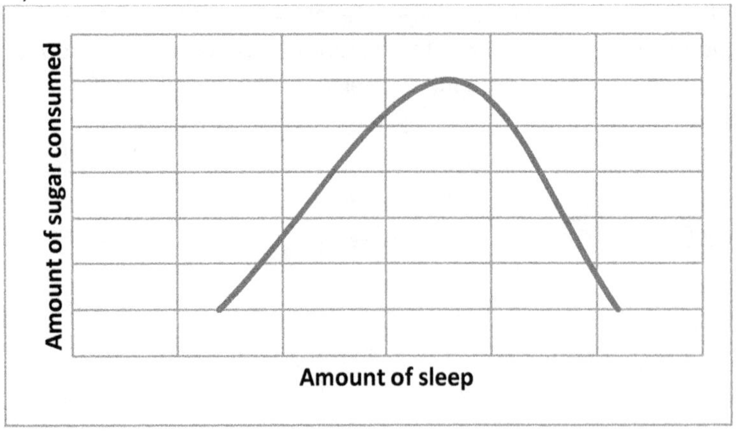
Amount of sugar consumed
Amount of sleep

Your exam will have problems like this one that show line graphs of linear equations. Be sure that you know the difference between positive linear relationships and negative linear relationships for the exam. In a positive linear relationship, an increase in one variable causes an increase in the other variable, meaning that the line will point upwards from left to right.

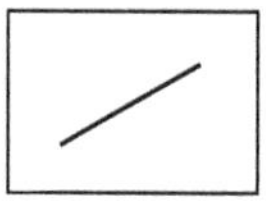

In a negative linear relationship, an increase in one variable causes a decrease in the other variable, meaning that the line will point downwards from left to right.

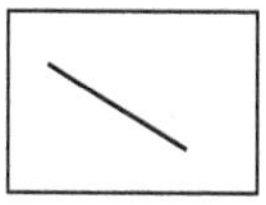

38) Which one of the scatterplots below most strongly suggests a negative linear relationship between x and y?

A)

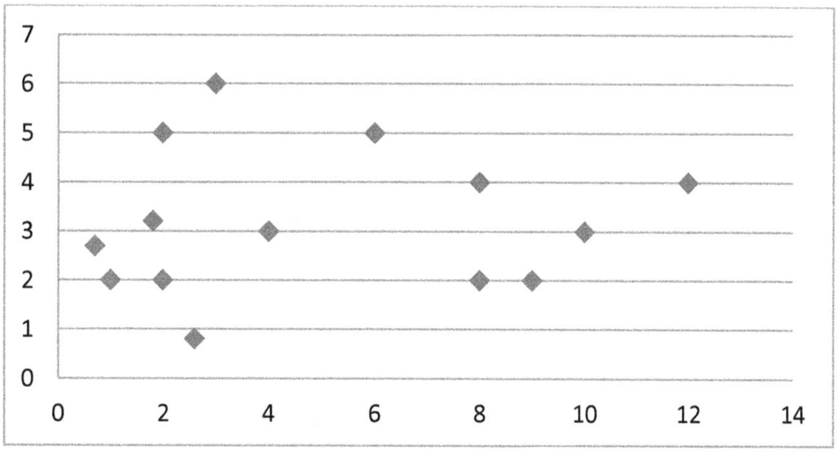

B)

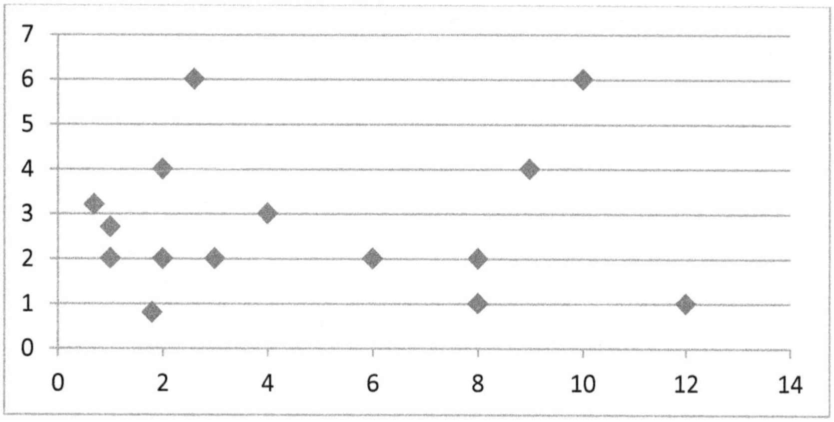

C)

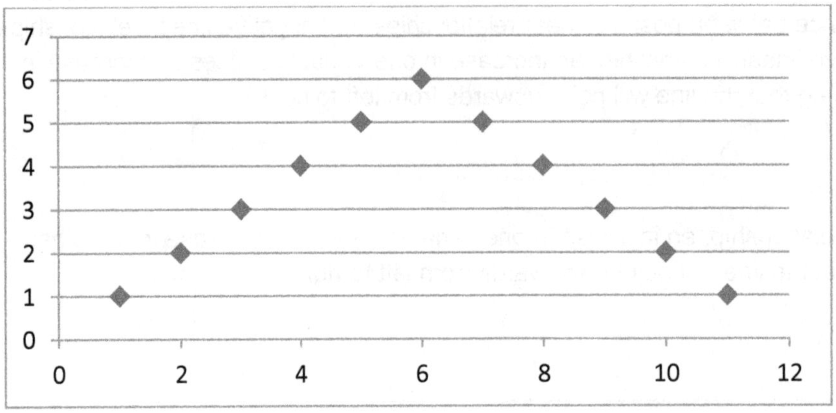

D)

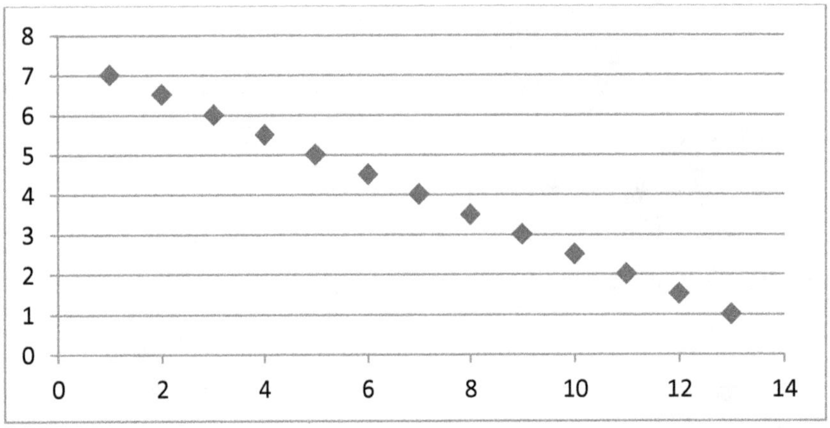

Your exam may have problems containing scatterplots like those above. For these types of questions, you will need to look at each scatterplot and determine which one has the dots in a configuration most similar to the one in the question. As stated in the previous problem, be sure that you know the difference between positive linear relationships and negative linear relationships for the exam. When the dots appear to be placed at random locations, we say that there is no relationship between x and y.

39) The graph of a linear equation is shown below. Which one of the tables of values best represents the points on the graph?

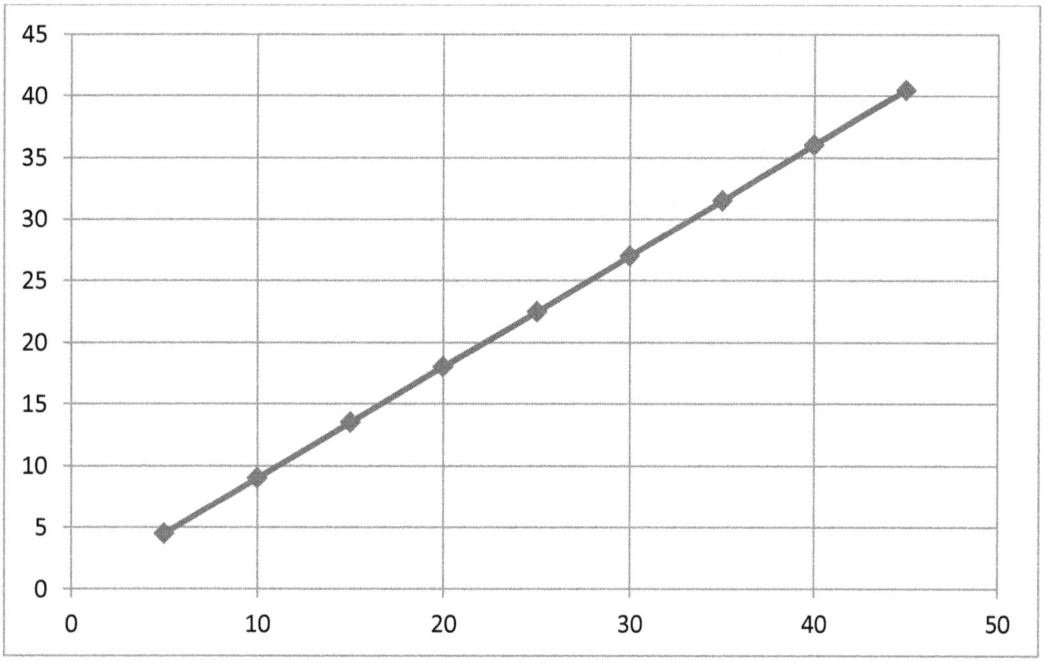

A)

x	y
5	5
10	10
15	15
20	20

B)

x	y
5	4
10	8
15	12
20	16

C)

x	y
5	4.5
10	9
15	13.5
20	18

D)

x	y
5	9
10	13
15	15
20	20

This is an example of an exam question on graphing that involves functions. A function expresses the mathematical relationship between x and y. Functions are expressed by using the notation: $f(x)$. To solve problems like this one, try to determine what recurring mathematical operation on x will yield a result of y. In this question, we have the function: $f(x) = x \times 0.9$. For instance, $f(x) = 5 \times 0.9 = 4.5$.

40)

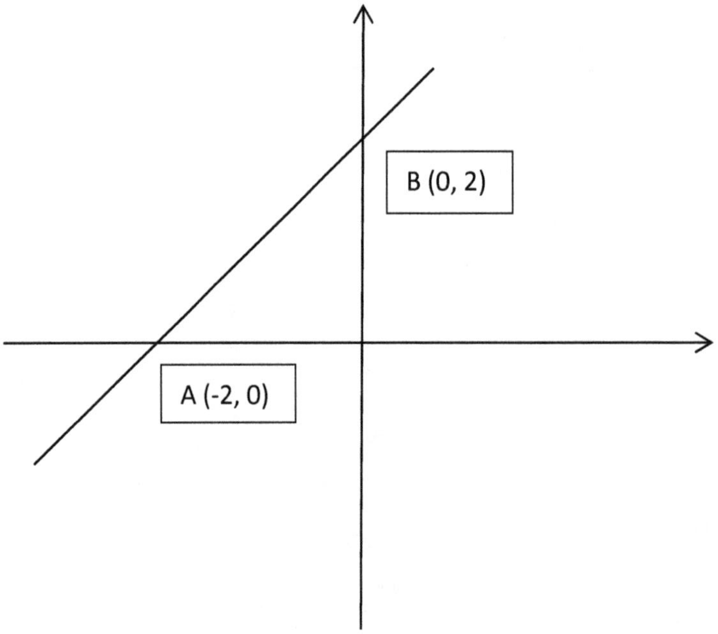

The line in the xy plane above is going to be shifted 5 units to the left and 4 units up. What are the coordinates of point B after the shift?

A) (–5, 6)
B) (5, 6)
C) (5, 4)
D) (–7, 4)

This question involves transposing the coordinates of a linear equation. Remember these rules on transpositions:
x coordinate moved to the left – deduct the units from the original x coordinate
x coordinate moved to the right – add the units to the original x coordinate
y coordinate moved down – deduct the units from the original y coordinate
y coordinate moved up – add the units to the original y coordinate

41) An airplane flew at a constant speed, traveling 780 miles in 2 hours. The graph below shows the total miles the airplane traveled in 20 minute intervals. According to the graph, how many miles did the plane travel in the last 40 minutes of its journey?

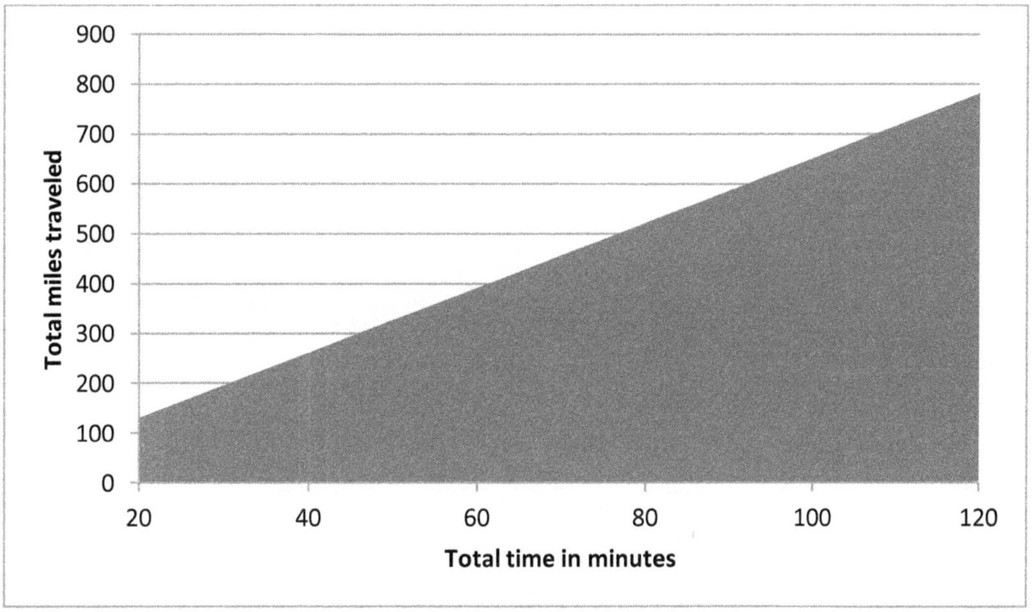

A) 120
B) 180
C) 200
D) 260

These types of problems will often have two variables. In the graph above, variable x is the total time and variable y is the total miles traveled. Try to find the function that expresses the relationship between the two variables.

42) What is the distance between (1,0) and (5,4)?

A) 4

B) $\sqrt{32}$

C) $\sqrt{18}$

D) 16

The distance formula is used to calculate the linear distance between two points on a two-dimensional graph. The two points are represented by the coordinates (x_1, y_1) and (x_2, y_2).

The distance formula is as follows:

$$d = \sqrt{(x_2 - x_1)^2 + (y_2 - y_1)^2}$$

43) The line on the xy-graph below forms the diameter of the circle. What is the approximate area of the circle?

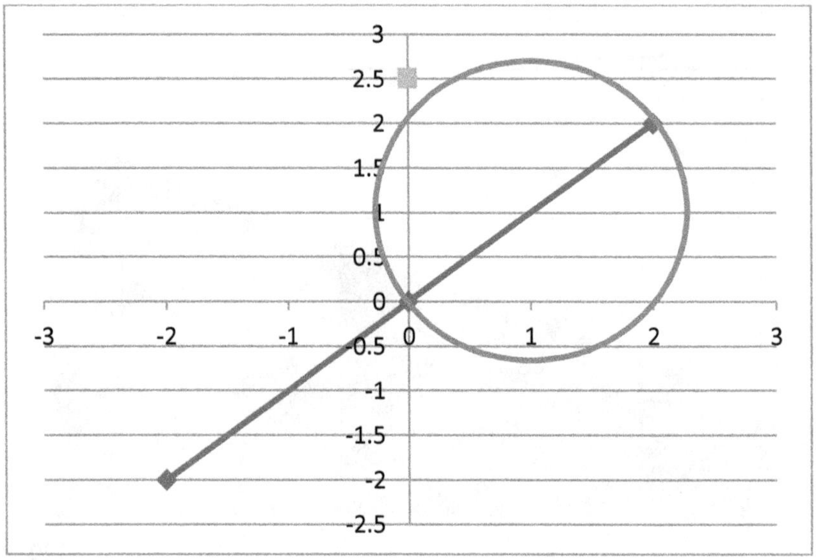

A) π
B) 2π
C) $\frac{\pi}{2}$
D) 2.5π

The question above is asking you to find the area of a circle that lies on the xy-coordinate plane. To solve the problem, you will need the formulas for hypotenuse length, radius, and area. The formulas are:

Area of a circle = $\pi R^2 = \pi \times \text{radius}^2$

Hypotenuse length: $\sqrt{A^2 + B^2} = C$

Radius of a circle = ½ × diameter

44) The diagram below depicts a cell phone tower. The height of the tower from point B at the center of its base to point T at the top is 30 meters, and the distance from point B of the tower to point A on the ground is 18 meters. What is the approximate distance from point A on the ground to the top (T) of the cell phone tower?

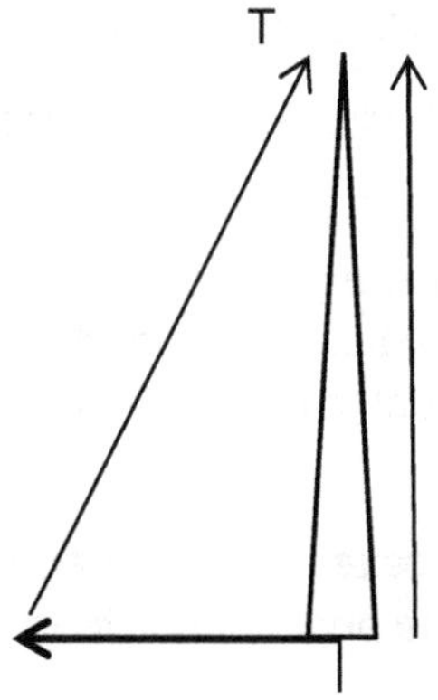

A) 10 meters
B) 20 meters
C) 30 meters
D) 35 meters

We need to use the Pythagorean Theorem to solve the problem. The Pythagorean Theorem deals with right triangles. The theorem helps us to calculate the length of the hypotenuse, which is the side opposite the right angle (The right angle is at the 90° corner of the triangle.) The hypotenuse is called side *C* in the formula for the Pythagorean Theorem. The theorem states that the length of the hypotenuse is equal to the square root of the sum of the squares of the lengths of the two other sides (A and B). So, we use the following formula to calculate the length of the hypotenuse:

$$\sqrt{A^2 + B^2} = C$$

45) Which of the following statements about isosceles triangles is true?

A) Isosceles triangles have two equal sides.
B) When an altitude is drawn in an isosceles triangle, two equilateral triangles are formed.
C) The base of an isosceles triangle must be shorter than the length of each of the other two sides.
D) The sum of the measurements of the interior angles of an isosceles triangle must be equal to 360°.

This question assesses your knowledge of the rules for triangles and angles. Remember these principles on angles and triangles for your exam:

The sum of all three angles in any triangle must be equal to 180 degrees.

An isosceles triangle has two equal sides and two equal angles.

An equilateral triangle has three equal sides and three equal angles.

Angles that have the same measurement in degrees are called congruent angles.

Equilateral triangles are sometimes called congruent triangles.

Two angles are supplementary if they add up to 180 degrees. This means that when the two angles are placed together, they will form a straight line on one side.

Two angles are complementary (sometimes called adjacent angles) if they add up to 90 degrees. This means that the two angles will form a right triangle.

When two parallel lines are cut by a transversal (a straight line that runs through both of the parallel lines), 4 pairs of opposite (non-adjacent) angles are formed and 4 pairs of corresponding angles are formed. The opposite angles will be equal in measure, and the corresponding angles will also be equal in measure.

A parallelogram is a four-sided figure in which opposite sides are parallel and equal in length. Each angle will have the same measurement as the angle opposite to it, so a parallelogram has two pairs of opposite angles.

The sides of a 30° - 60° - 90° triangle are in the ratio of 1: $\sqrt{3}$: 2.

46) The figure below shows a right triangular prism. Side AB measures 3.5 units, side AC measures 4 units, and side BD measures 5 units. What amount below best approximates the total surface area of this triangular prism in square units?

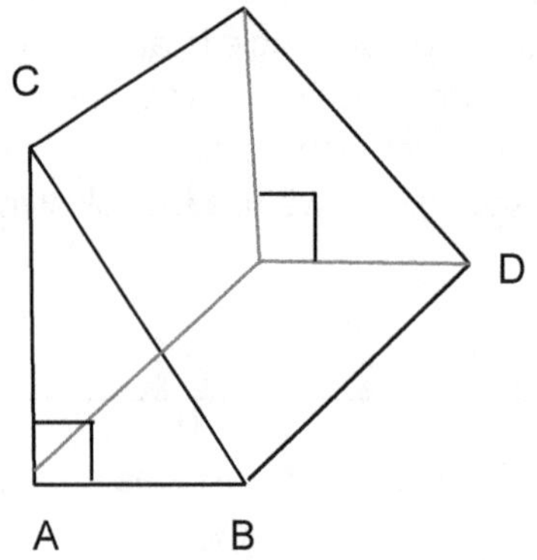

A) 66.5
B) 72.85
C) 74
D) 78.00

This question is evaluating your knowledge of how to calculate the surface area of a right triangular prism, which is composed of both rectangles and triangles. You will again need the Pythagorean Theorem, as well as the formulas for the areas of rectangles and triangles: Area of a rectangle = L × W = Length × Width; Area of a triangle = $bH \div 2$ = base × height ÷ 2

47) Which of the following dimensions would be needed in order to find the area of the figure?

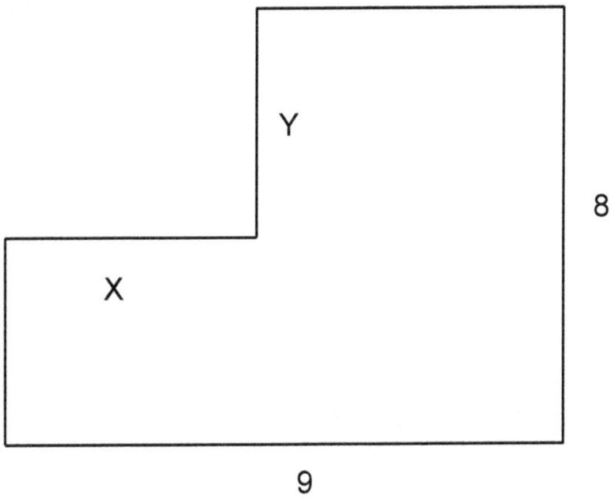

A) X only
B) Y only
C) Both X and Y
D) Either X or Y

This question is asking you to calculate the area of a hybrid shape. To solve problems like this one, try to visualize two rectangles. The first rectangle would measure 8 × 9 and the second rectangle would measure X × Y.

48) The area of a square is 64 square units. This square is made up of smaller squares that measure 4 square units each. How many of the smaller squares are needed to make up the larger square?
A) 8
B) 12
C) 16
D) 24

This question is asking you to determine the relationships between square figures of different sizes. For problems about placing small squares inside a larger square, you can simply divide the size of the smaller squares into the size of the larger square in order to determine how many small squares are required.

49) The base (B) of the cylinder in the illustration shown below is at a right angle to its sides. The radius (R) of the base of cylinder measures 5 centimeters. A circular plane that is perpendicular to the base is placed inside the cylinder. Which of the following could be true about this perpendicular circular plane?

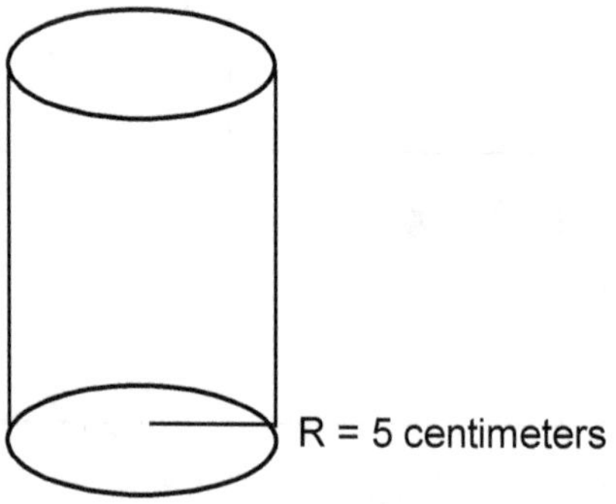

A) Its radius is equal to R.
B) Its radius is greater than 5.
C) Its radius is greater than 10.
D) It will be double the size of B.

This question is asking you to interpret relationships between cylindrical and circular figures. In this question, the relationship involves right angle geometry. Remember that if two planes are perpendicular, a right angle is formed where the two planes meet. If two planes form a right angle within a cylinder, then the radius of the base of the cylinder will need to be equal to or greater than the radius of the figure that is to be inserted into the cylinder.

Although not needed for this problem, you should also learn the formula to calculate the volume of a cylinder:

$$\text{Volume of cylinder} = \pi R^2 h = \pi \times radius^2 \times height$$

50) The illustration below shows a right circular cone. The entire cone has a base radius of 9 and a height of 18.

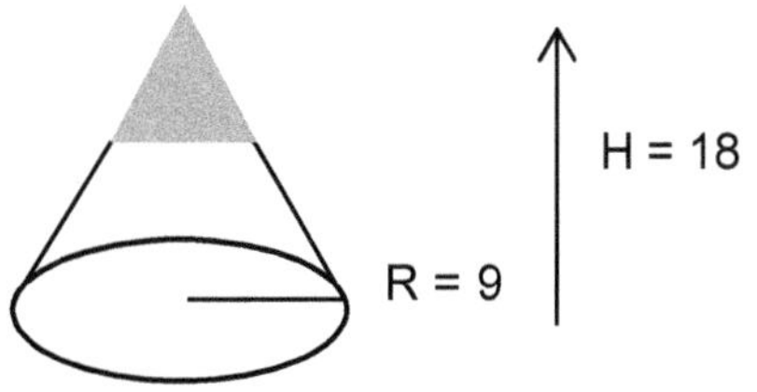

The shaded portion at the top of the cone has a height of 6. What fraction expresses the volume of the shaded portion to the volume of the entire cone?

A) $^1/_{27}$
B) $^2/_{27}$
C) $^1/_3$
D) $^1/_6$

This question is asking you to calculate the volume of a cone. The formula for the volume of a cone is:

$$\frac{\pi R^2 H}{3}$$

(π × radius squared × height) ÷ 3

Although not needed for this problem, you will also need to know how to calculate the volume of a pyramid for your exam. The volume of a pyramid is calculated by taking one-third of the base area times the height:

Volume of a pyramid: $Base\ area \times H \times \frac{1}{3}$

TABE Practice Math Test 2 – Answer Key

1) A
2) A
3) B
4) D
5) C
6) C
7) B
8) B
9) A
10) A
11) C
12) C
13) A
14) C
15) D
16) C
17) B
18) C
19) C
20) A
21) D
22) D
23) C
24) B
25) A
26) C
27) B
28) A
29) C
30) B
31) D
32) B
33) D
34) A
35) A

36) B

37) C

38) D

39) C

40) A

41) D

42) B

43) B

44) D

45) A

46) D

47) C

48) C

49) A

50) A

TABE Practice Math Test 2 – Solutions and Explanations

1) The correct answer is A. Remember the two concepts: (a) Negative numbers are less than positive numbers; (b) When two fractions have the same numerator, the fraction with the smaller number in the denominator is the larger fraction. So, $-{}^{1}/_{4}$ is less than ${}^{1}/_{8}$, ${}^{1}/_{8}$ is less than ${}^{1}/_{6}$, and ${}^{1}/_{6}$ is less than 1.

2) The correct answer is A. From the facts in the problem, we know that η needs to be greater than ${}^{25}/_{13}$. If we convert ${}^{25}/_{13}$ to decimal form, we get 1.923077. The square root of 36 is 6, so (A) is the correct response because it is greater than1.923077.

3) The correct answer is B. 7*x* is between 5 and 6, so set up an inequality as follows:
$5 < 7x < 6$

Then insert the fractions from the answer choices for the value of x to solve the problem.
$5 < (7 \times {}^{3}/_{4}) < 6$
$5 < [(7 \times 3) \div 4] < 6$
$5 < (21 \div 4) < 6$
$5 < 5.25 < 6$
5.25 is between 5 and 6, so ${}^{3}/_{4}$ is the correct answer.

4) The correct answer is D. First of all, you need to determine the difference in temperature during the entire time period: 62 – 38 = 24 degrees less

Then calculate how much time has passed. From 5:00 PM to 11:00 PM, 6 hours have passed. Next, divide the temperature difference by the amount of time that has passed to get the temperature change per hour: 24 degrees ÷ 6 hours = 4 degrees less per hour

To calculate the temperature at the stated time, you need to calculate the time difference. From 5:00 PM to 9:00 PM, 4 hours have passed. So, the temperature difference during the stated time is 4 hours × 4 degrees per hour = 16 degrees less.

Finally, deduct this from the beginning temperature to get your final answer: 62° F – 16° F = 46° F

5) The correct answer is C. The number of hot dogs is *D* and the number of hamburgers is *H*. The equation to express the problem is: (D × \$2.50) + (H × \$4) = \$22
We know that the number of hamburgers is 3, so put that in the equation and solve it.
(D × \$2.50) + (H × \$4) = \$22
(D × \$2.50) + (3 × \$4) = \$22
(D × \$2.50) + 12 = \$22
(D × \$2.50) + 12 – 12 = \$22 – 12
(D × \$2.50) = \$10
\$2.50D = \$10
\$2.50D ÷ \$2.50 = \$10 ÷ \$2.50
$D = 4$

6) The correct answer is C. For your first step, determine how many square feet there are in total: 2000 square feet per room × 8 rooms = 16,000 square feet in total

Then you need to divide by the coverage rate:
16,000 square feet to cover ÷ 900 square feet coverage per bucket = 17.77 buckets needed

It is not possible to purchase a partial bucket of paint, so 17.77 is rounded up to 18 buckets of paint.

7) The correct answer is B. Divide the distance traveled by the time in order to get the speed in miles per hour. Remember that in order to divide by a fraction, you need to invert the fraction, and then multiply.
3.6 miles ÷ $^3/_4$ =
3.6 × $^4/_3$ =
(3.6 × 4) ÷ 3 =
14.4 ÷ 3 = 4.8 miles per hour

8) The correct answer is B. To determine the number of combinations of *S* at a time that can be made from a set containing *N* items, you need this formula: $(N!) \div [(N - S)! \times S!]$ In our question, $S = 2$ and $N = 5$ (because there are five letters in the set). So, substitute the values for *S* and *N*:
$(5 \times 4 \times 3 \times 2 \times 1) \div [(5 - 2)! \times (2!)] = (5 \times 4 \times 3 \times 2) \div [(3 \times 2 \times 1) \times (2 \times 1)] = 120 \div 12 = 10$

9) The correct answer is A. In order to calculate the number of permutations of size *S* taken from *N* items, you should use this formula: $N! \div (N - S)!$ In our problem, $N = 5$ and $S = 4$
$N! \div (N - S)! = (5 \times 4 \times 3 \times 2 \times 1) \div (5 - 4) = (5 \times 4 \times 3 \times 2) \div 1 = 120 \div 1 = 120$

10) The correct answer is A. The mode is the number that occurs the most frequently in the set. Our data set is: 1, 1, 3, 2, 4, 3, 1, 2, 1. The number 1 occurs 4 times in the set, which is more frequently than any other number in the set, so the mode is 1.

11) The correct answer is C. To calculate the range, the low number in the set is deducted from the high number in the set. The problem set is: 98.5, 85.5, 80.0, 97, 93, 92.5, 93, 87, 88, 82. The high number is 98.5 and the low number is 80, so the range is 18.5 (98.5 – 80 = 18.5).

12) The correct answer is C. The mean is the average of all of the numbers in the set. If we look at each of the answers, we can see that we have seven values in each set because there are seven dots above each of the number lines. The mean for answer choice C is 4.57 and the median is 5.
Mean: 1 + 2 + 3 + 5 + 6 + 7 + 8 = 32; 32 ÷7 = 4.57
Median: 1, 2, 3, **5**, 6, 7, 8
So, the median exceeds the mean for the set represented on number line (C).

13) The correct answer is A. Find the total of the items in the sample space:
5 + 10 + 8 + 12 = 35.
We want to know the chance of getting an orange balloon, so put that in the denominator: $\frac{10}{35} = \frac{2}{7}$

14) The correct answer is C. For ten sandwiches, the total price is \$85, so each sandwich sells for \$8.50: \$85 total sales in dollars ÷ 10 sandwiches sold = \$8.50 each

15) The correct answer is D. Ten out of 25 students participate in drama club. First of all, express the relationship as a fraction: $^{10}/_{25}$

Then divide to find the percentage: $^{10}/_{25} = 10 \div 25 = 0.40 = 40\%$

Finally, choose the pie chart that has 40% of its area shaded in dark gray.

40% is slightly less than half, so you need to choose chart D.

16) The correct answer is C. The quantity of diseases is indicated on the bottom of the graph, while the number of children is indicated on the left side of the graph. To determine the amount of children that have been vaccinated against three or more diseases, we need to add the amounts represented by the bars for 3, 4, and 5 diseases: 30 + 20 + 10 = 60 children

17) The correct answer is B. Remember that the number before the times sign has to be between 1 and 10. So, we have to move the decimal four places to the left to get 1.9875246. Since we have moved the decimal four places, we use 4 as our exponent:
1.9875246×10^4

In other words, you can check your work as follows: The exponent correlates to the amount of zeroes that are to be placed after the 1 when we multiply the power of ten.

$10^4 = 10 \times 10 \times 10 \times 10 = 10{,}000$
$1.9875246 \times 10{,}000 = 19{,}875.246$

18) The correct answer is C. At the beginning of the year, 15% of the 1,500 creatures were fish, so there were 225 fish at the beginning of the year (1,500 × 0.15 = 225).

In order to find the percentage of fish at the end of the year, we first need to add up the percentages for the other animals: 40% + 23% + 21% = 84%

Then subtract this amount from 100% to get the remaining percentage for the fish:
100% – 84% = 16%

Multiply the percentage by the total to get the number of fish at the end of the year:
1,500 × 0.16 = 240

Then subtract the beginning of the year from the end of the year to calculate the increase in the number of fish: 240 – 225 = 15

19) The correct answer is C. Isolate the integers to one side of the equation.

$$\frac{3}{4}x - 2 = 4$$

$$\frac{3}{4}x - 2 + 2 = 4 + 2$$

$$\frac{3}{4}x = 6$$

Then get rid of the fraction by multiplying both sides by the denominator.

$$\frac{3}{4}x \times 4 = 6 \times 4$$

$$3x = 24$$

Then divide to solve the problem.
$3x \div 3 = 24 \div 3$
$x = 8$

20) The correct answer is A.

Perform the multiplication on the terms in the parentheses.
$2(3x - 1) = 4(x + 1) - 3$
$6x - 2 = (4x + 4) - 3$

Then simplify.
$6x - 2 = (4x + 4) - 3$
$6x - 2 = 4x + 1$
$6x - 2 - 1 = 4x + 1 - 1$
$6x - 3 = 4x$

Then isolate x to get your answer.
$6x - 3 = 4x$
$6x - 4x - 3 = 4x - 4x$
$2x - 3 = 0$
$2x - 3 + 3 = 0 + 3$
$2x = 3$
$2x \div 2 = 3 \div 2$
$x = {}^{3}/_{2}$

21) The correct answer is D. Factor each of the parentheticals in the expression provided in the problem:
$(3x + 3y)(5a + 5b) =$
$3(x + y) \times 5(a + b)$

We know that $x + y = 5$ and $a + b = 4$, so we can substitute the values stated for each of the parentheticals:
$3(x + y) \times 5(a + b) =$
$3(5) \times 5(4) =$
$15 \times 20 = 300$

22) The correct answer is D. Place the integers on one side of the inequality.
$-3x + 14 < 5$
$-3x + 14 - 14 < 5 - 14$
$-3x < -9$

Then get rid of the negative number. We need to reverse the way that the inequality sign points because we are dividing by a negative.
$-3x < -9$
$-3x \div -3 > -9 \div -3$ ("Less than" becomes "greater than" because we divide by a negative number.)
$x > 3$
4.35 is greater than 3, so it is the correct answer.

23) The correct answer is C. In order to solve inequalities, deal with the whole numbers on each side of the equation first.

$20 - \frac{3x}{4} \geq 17$

$(20 - 20) - \frac{3x}{4} \geq 17 - 20$

$-\frac{3x}{4} \geq -3$

Then deal with the fraction.

$-\frac{3x}{4} \geq -3$

$\left(4 \times -\frac{3x}{4}\right) \geq -3 \times 4$

$-3x \geq -12$

Then deal with the remaining whole numbers.

$-3x \geq -12$

$-3x \div 3 \geq -12 \div 3$

$-x \geq -4$

Then deal with the negative number.

$-x \geq -4$

$-x + 4 \geq -4 + 4$

$-x + 4 \geq 0$

Finally, isolate the unknown variable as a positive number.

$-x + 4 \geq 0$

$-x + x + 4 \geq 0 + x$

$4 \geq x$

$x \leq 4$

24) The correct answer is B. You need to find the lowest common denominator. Then add the numerators together as shown.

$\frac{x}{5} + \frac{y}{2} =$

$\left(\frac{x}{5} \times \frac{2}{2}\right) + \left(\frac{y}{2} \times \frac{5}{5}\right) =$

$$\frac{2x}{10}+\frac{5y}{10}=$$

$$\frac{2x+5y}{10}$$

25) The correct answer is A. Multiply each side of the equation by *Z*. Then divide by *W* in order to isolate *Z*.

$$W=\frac{XY}{Z}$$

$$W\times Z=\frac{XY}{Z}\times Z$$

$$WZ=XY$$

$$WZ\div W=XY\div W$$

$$Z=\frac{XY}{W}$$

26) The correct answer is C. Shanika wants to earn $4,000 this month. She gets the $1,000 basic pay regardless of the number of cars she sells, so we need to subtract that from the total first: $4,000 – $1,000 = $3,000

She gets $390 for each car she sells, so we need to divide that into the remaining $3,000:
$3,000 to earn ÷ $390 per car = 7.69 cars to sell

Since it is not possible to sell a part of a car, we need to round up to 8 cars.

Alternatively, we could have solved the problem by using the following algebraic expression:
$4,000 = $1,000 + ($390 × *x*)
$3,000 ÷ $390 = *x*

27) The correct answer is B. Place the base number inside the radical sign. The denominator of the exponent is the nth root of the radical. The numerator is the new exponent: $x^{4/9}=(\sqrt[9]{x})^4$

28) The correct answer is A. The total amount that Toby has to pay is represented by C. He is paying D dollars immediately, so we can determine the remaining amount that he owes by deducting his down payment from the total. So, the remaining amount owing is represented by the equation: C – D

We have to divide the remaining amount owing by the number of months (M) to get the monthly payment (P): P = (C – D) ÷ M = $\frac{C-D}{M}$

29) The correct answer is C. The amount of time in hours (*T*) multiplied by miles per hour (mph) gives us the distance traveled (*D*). So, the equation for distance traveled is: *T* × mph = *D*

The problem tells us that we need to calculate *T*, so we need to isolate *T* by changing our equation as follows:
T × mph = *D*
(*T* × mph) ÷ mph = *D* ÷ mph

$T = D \div \text{mph}$

In our problem, Fatima drives home on the same route that she took into town, so we need to calculate the traveling time for the journey into town, as well as for the journey home:
$(D \div 50) + (D \div 60) = T$

Then add back the 20 minutes she spent in town to get the total time:
$Tt = [(D \div 50) + (D \div 60)] + 20 \text{ minutes}$

30) The correct answer is B. We need to set up a fraction, the numerator of which consists of the amount of sales in dollars for sweatpants, and the denominator of which consists of the total amount of sales in dollars for both items. The problem tells us that the amount of sales in dollars for sweatpants is 30*s* and the total amount of sales is 850, so the answer is 30*s*/850.

31) The correct answer is D.

Step 1: Apply the distributive property of multiplication by multiplying the item in front of the opening parenthesis by each item inside the pair of parentheses.

Step 2: Add up the individual products in order to solve the problem.

$$10ab^5(5ab^7 - 4b^3 - 10a) =$$

$$(10ab^5 \times 5ab^7) - (10ab^5 \times 4b^3) - (10ab^5 \times 10a) =$$
$$50a^2b^{12} - 40ab^8 - 100a^2b^5$$

32) The correct answer is B.

STEP 1: The numerator of the first fraction is $x^2 + 10x + 16$, so the final integer is 16.

The factors of 16 are:
1 × 16 = 16
2 × 8 = 16
4 × 4 = 16

Then add these factors together to discover what integer you need to use in front of the second term of the expression.
1 + 16 = 17
2 + 8 = 10
4 + 4 = 8

2 and 8 satisfy both parts of the equation.

Therefore, the factors of $x^2 + 10x + 16$ are $(x+2)(x+8)$.

Now factor the other parts of the problem.

STEP 2: The denominator of the first fraction is $x^2 + 11x + 18$, so the final integer is 18.
The factors of 18 are:
1 × 18 = 18
2 × 9 = 18
3 × 6 = 18

Add these factors together to find the integer to use in front of the second term of the expression.
1 + 18 = 19

2 + 9 = 11
3 + 6 = 9
Therefore, the factors of $x^2+11x+18$ are $(x+2)(x+9)$.

STEP 3: The numerator of the second fraction is x^2+9x, so there is no final integer.
Because x is common to both terms of the expression, the factor will be in this format:
$x(x+\quad)$
Therefore, the factors of x^2+9x are $x(x+9)$.

STEP 4: The denominator of the second fraction is $x^2+17x+72$, so the final integer is 72.
The factors of 72 are:
1 × 72 = 72
2 × 36 = 72
3 × 24 = 72
4 × 18 = 72
6 × 12 = 72
8 × 9 = 72

Add these factors together to find the integer to use in front of the second term of the expression.
1 + 72 = 73
2 + 36 = 38
3 + 24 = 27
4 + 18 = 22
6 + 12 = 18
8 + 9 = 17

Therefore, the factors of $x^2+17x+72$ are $(x+8)(x+9)$.

Now we can solve our problem with the factors that we have found in each step.

$$\frac{x^2+10x+16}{x^2+11x+18}=\frac{(x+2)(x+8)}{(x+2)(x+9)} \qquad \frac{x^2+9x}{x^2+17x+72}=\frac{x(x+9)}{(x+8)(x+9)}$$

So, replace the polynomials in the question with their factors from above.

$$\frac{x^2+10x+16}{x^2+11x+18}\times\frac{x^2+9x}{x^2+17x+72}=$$

$$\frac{(x+2)(x+8)}{(x+2)(x+9)}\times\frac{x(x+9)}{(x+8)(x+9)}$$

Then for each fraction, you need to simplify by removing the common factors.

Remove $(x+2)$ from the first fraction.

$$\frac{(x+2)(x+8)}{(x+2)(x+9)}\times\frac{x(x+9)}{(x+8)(x+9)}=$$

$$\frac{(x+8)}{(x+9)} \times \frac{x(x+9)}{(x+8)(x+9)}$$

Then remove $(x + 9)$ from the second fraction.

$$\frac{(x+8)}{(x+9)} \times \frac{x(x+9)}{(x+8)(x+9)} =$$

$$\frac{(x+8)}{(x+9)} \times \frac{x}{(x+8)}$$

Once you have simplified each fraction as above, perform the operation indicated. In this problem, you need to multiply the two fractions.

$$\frac{(x+8)}{(x+9)} \times \frac{x}{(x+8)} = \frac{x(x+8)}{(x+9)(x+8)}$$

When you have completed the operation, you need to check to see whether any further simplification is possible.

In this case, the fraction may be further simplified because the numerator and denominator share the common factor $(x + 8)$.

$$\frac{x(x+8)}{(x+9)(x+8)} = \frac{x}{x+9}$$

So, our final answer is $\frac{x}{x+9}$

33) The correct answer is D. When dividing fractions, you need to invert the second fraction and then multiply the two fractions together.

$$\frac{5z-5}{z} \div \frac{6z-6}{5z^2} =$$

$$\frac{5z-5}{z} \times \frac{5z^2}{6z-6}$$

When multiplying fractions, you multiply the numerator of the first fraction by the numerator of the second fraction and denominator of the first fraction by the denominator of the second fraction.

$$\frac{5z-5}{z} \times \frac{5z^2}{6z-6} =$$

$$\frac{5z^2(5z-5)}{z(6z-6)} =$$

$$\frac{25z^3 - 25z^2}{6z^2 - 6z}$$

Then look at the numerator and denominator from the result of the previous step to see if you can factor and simplify.

In this case, the numerator and denominator have the common factor of $(z^2 - z)$.

$$\frac{25z^3 - 25z^2}{6z^2 - 6z} =$$

$$\frac{25z(z^2 - z)}{6(z^2 - z)} =$$

$$\frac{25z}{6}$$

34) The correct answer is A. We know that 2 inches represents *F* feet. We can set this up as the ratio 2/*F*.

Next, we need to calculate the ratio for *F* + 1. The number of inches that represents *F* + 1 is unknown, so we will refer to this unknown as *x*. So we have:

$$\frac{2}{F} = \frac{x}{F+1}$$

Now cross multiply.

$$\frac{2}{F} = \frac{x}{F+1}$$

$$F \times x = 2 \times (F + 1)$$

$$Fx = 2(F + 1)$$

Then isolate *x* to solve.

$$Fx \div F = [2(F + 1)] \div F$$

$$x = \frac{2(F+1)}{F}$$

35) The correct answer is A. We know from the original graph in the question that when *x* is a positive number, then *y* will also be positive. This is represented by the curve in the upper right-hand quadrant of the graph.

We also know from the original graph in the question that when *x* is negative, *y* will also be negative. This is represented by the curve in the lower left-hand quadrant of the graph.

If we add the absolute value symbols to the problem, then $|(x - 4)|$ will always result in a positive value for *y*.

Therefore, even when *x* is negative, *y* will be positive.

So, the curve originally represented in the lower left-hand quadrant of the graph must be shifted into the upper left-hand quadrant.

36) The correct answer is B.

Isolate the unknown variable in order to solve the problem.

$-3x > 6$

$-3x \div 3 > 6 \div 3$

$-x > 2$

In order to solve the problem, we have to multiply each side of the inequality by –1.

When we multiply both sides of an inequality by a negative number, we have to reverse the greater than symbol to a less than symbol (or if there is a less than symbol, we reverse it to a greater than symbol).

$-x \times -1 < 2 \times -1$

$x < -2$

In other words, if the isolated variable is negative as in this problem, you need to reverse the greater than symbol in order to make it the less than symbol.

$-x > 2$

$x < -2$

This is represented by line B.

37) The correct answer is C. As the quantity of sugar increases, the amount of sleep also increases. A positive linear relationship therefore exists between the two variables. This is represented in chart C since the amount of sleep is greater when the amount of sugar consumed is higher.

38) The correct answer is D. A negative linear relationship exists when an increase in one variable results in a decrease in the other variable. This is represented by chart D.

39) The correct answer is C. We can see that the line does not begin on exactly on (5, 5), nor does it begin on (5, 9) because the first point is slightly below the horizontal line for $y = 5$. Therefore, we can rule out answers A and D.

If we look at $x = 20$ on the graph, we can see that $y = 18$ at this point.
As stated in the study tip, we can express this as the function: $f(x) = x \times 0.9$

Putting in the values of x from chart (C), we get the following:
$5 \times 0.9 = 4.5$
$10 \times 0.9 = 9$
$15 \times 0.9 = 13.5$
$20 \times 0.9 = 18$

40) The correct answer is A. We start off with point B, which is represented by the coordinates (0, 2). The line is then shifted 5 units to the left and 4 units up. When we go to the left, we need to deduct the units, and when we go up we need to add units. So, do the operations on each of the coordinates in order to solve: $0 - 5 = -5$ and $2 + 4 = 6$, so our new coordinates are (–5, 6).

41) The correct answer is D. The last 40 minutes of the journey begin at the 80 minute mark and end at the 120 minute mark. The line for 80 minutes is at 520 miles and the line for 120 minutes is at 780 miles, so the plane has traveled 260 miles (780 – 520 = 260) in the last 40 minutes.

Alternatively, we can use the function that this graph represents to solve the problem.
First, we can perform division to determine that the plane travels 6.5 miles per minute.

For example, the line for 120 minutes is at 780 miles:

780 miles ÷ 120 minutes = 6.5 miles per minute

$$f(x) = x \times 6.5 = 40 \times 6.5 = 260$$

42) The correct answer is B. The distance formula is used to calculate the linear distance between two points on a two-dimensional graph. The two points are represented by the coordinates (x_1, y_1) and (x_2, y_2).

The distance formula is as follows: $d = \sqrt{(x_2 - x_1)^2 + (y_2 - y_1)^2}$

Substitute values into the distance formula from the facts stated in the problem.

$d = \sqrt{(x_2 - x_1)^2 + (y_2 - y_1)^2}$

$d = \sqrt{(5-1)^2 + (4-0)^2}$

$d = \sqrt{4^2 + 4^2}$

$d = \sqrt{16 + 16}$

$d = \sqrt{32}$

43) The correct answer is B. The line that represents the diameter of the circle forms the hypotenuse of a triangle. Side A of the triangle begins on (0, 0) and ends on (0, 2), with a length of 2. Side B of the triangle begins on (0, 2) and ends on (2, 2), so it also has a length of 2. So, the diameter of the circle is: $\sqrt{2^2 + 2^2} = \sqrt{8} = 2\sqrt{2}$

Next, we need to calculate the radius of the circle. The radius of the circle is $\sqrt{2}$ because the diameter is $2\sqrt{2}$ and the formula for the radius of a circle is ½ × diameter = radius.

Finally, we can use the formula for the area of a circle to solve the problem:

$\pi\sqrt{2}^2 = 2\pi$

44) The correct answer is D. In our problem we know that one side of the triangle is 18 meters and the other side of the triangle is 30 meters, so we can put these values into the formula in order to solve the problem.

$\sqrt{A^2 + B^2} = C$

$\sqrt{18^2 + 30^2} = C$

$\sqrt{324 + 900} = C$

$\sqrt{1224} = C$

35 × 35 = 1225

So, the square root of 1224 is approximately 35.

$35 \approx C$

45) The correct answer is A. An isosceles triangle has two equal sides, so answer A is correct.

If an altitude is drawn in an isosceles triangle, we have to put a straight line down the middle of the triangle from the peak to the base. Dividing the triangle in this way would form two right triangles, rather than two equilateral triangles. So, answer B is incorrect.

The base of an isosceles triangle can be longer than the length of each of the other two sides, so answer C is incorrect.

The sum of all three angles of any triangle must be 180 degrees, rather than 360 degrees. So, answer D is incorrect.

By definition a triangle must have three sides. Also remember that all three angles inside the triangle must add up to 180 degrees and that right angles measure 90 degrees.

46) The correct answer is D. The prism has 5 sides, so we need to calculate the surface area of each one.

The rectangle at the bottom of the prism that lies along points, A, B, and D measures 3.5 units (side AB) by 5 units (side BD), so the surface area of the bottom rectangle is:

Length × Width = $3.5 \times 5 = 17.5$

Then calculate the area of the rectangle at the back of the triangle, lying along points A and C. This rectangle measures 4 units (side AC) by 5 units (the side that is parallel to side BD). So, the area of this side is:

Length × Width = $4 \times 5 = 20$

Next we need to find the length of the hypotenuse (side CB). Since AB is 3.5 units and AC is 4 units, we can use the Pythagorean Theorem as follows:

$\sqrt{3.5^2 + 4^2} = \sqrt{12.25 + 16} = \sqrt{28.25} \approx 5.3$

We can then calculate the surface area of the sloping rectangle that lies along the hypotenuse (along points C, B and D) as:

Length × Width = $5.3 \times 5 = 26.5$

Next, we need to calculate the surface area of the two triangles on each end of the prism. The formula for the area of a triangle is $bH \div 2$, so substituting the values we get:

$(3.5 \times 4) \div 2 = 7$

Finally, add the area of all five sides together to get the surface area for the entire prism:
$17.5 + 20 + 26.5 + 7 + 7 = 78$

47) The correct answer is C. Essentially a rectangle is missing at the upper left-hand corner of the figure. We would need to know both the length and width of the "missing" rectangle in order to calculate the area of our figure. So, we need to know both X and Y in order to solve the problem.

48) The correct answer is C. We simply divide to get the answer: 64 ÷ 4 = 16

49) The correct answer is A. The circular plane is perpendicular to the base of the cylinder, so a right angle is formed. Therefore, the perpendicular circular plane would need to be equal or lesser in size to the bottom of the cylinder in order for it to fit inside the cylinder. So, the radius of

the perpendicular circular plane would need to be equal to or less than the radius of the base of the cylinder. Therefore, the radius of the perpendicular cylinder could be equal to R.

50) The correct answers is A. First, we need to calculate the volume of the entire cone.

$(\pi \times 9^2 \times 18) \div 3 = 486\pi$

Then, we need to calculate the radius of the shaded portion. Since the height of the shaded portion is 6 and the height of the entire cone is 18, we know by using the rules of similarity that the ratio of the radius of the shaded portion to the radius of the entire cone is $^6/_{18}$ or $^1/_3$. Using this fraction, we can calculate the radius for the shaded portion. The radius of the entire cone is 9, so the radius of the shaded portion is 3.

$9 \times {}^1/_3 = 3$

Then, calculate the volume of the shaded portion.

$(\pi \times 3^2 \times 6) \div 3 = 18\pi$

So, we can express the volume of the shaded portion to the volume of the entire cone as: $^{18}/_{486}$

We then simplify this to $^1/_{27}$.

TABE Practice Math Test 3

Number and data problems:

1) Which of the following is the greatest?
A) 0.540
B) 0.054
C) 0.045
D) 0.5045

2) Farmer Brown has a field in which cows craze. He is going to buy fence panels to put up a fence along one side of the field. Each panel is 8 feet 6 inches long. He needs 11 panels to cover the entire side of the field. How long is the field?
A) 60 feet 6 inches
B) 72 feet 8 inches
C) 93 feet 6 inches
D) 102 feet 8 inches

3) If the value of x is between 0.0007 and 0.0021, which of the following could be x?
A) 0.0012
B) 0.0006
C) 0.0022
D) 0.022

4) The total funds, represented by variable F, available for P charity projects is represented by the equation F = \$500P + \$3,700. If the charity has \$40,000 available for projects, what is the greatest number of projects that can be completed?
A) 72
B) 73
C) 74
D) 79

5) Which of the following shows the numbers ordered from greatest to least?
A) $-{}^{1}/_{3}$, ${}^{1}/_{7}$, 1 , ${}^{1}/_{5}$
B) $-{}^{1}/_{3}$, ${}^{1}/_{5}$, ${}^{1}/_{7}$, 1
C) $-{}^{1}/_{3}$, 1 , ${}^{1}/_{7}$, ${}^{1}/_{5}$
D) 1 , ${}^{1}/_{5}$, ${}^{1}/_{7}$, $-{}^{1}/_{3}$

6) The students at Lyndon High School have been asked about their plans to attend the Homecoming Dance. The chart below shows the responses of each grade level by percentages. Which figure below best approximates the percentage of the total number of students from all four grades who will attend the dance? Note that each grade level has roughly the same number of students.

	Will Attend	**Will Not Attend**	**Undecided**
Freshmen:	45%	24%	31%
Sophomores:	30%	45%	25%
Juniors:	38%	20%	42%
Seniors:	30%	25%	45%

A) 25%
B) 35%
C) 45%
D) 55%

7) During each flight, a flight attendant must count the number of passengers on board the aircraft. The morning flight had 52 passengers more than the evening flight, and there were 540 passengers in total on the two flights that day. How many passengers were there on the evening flight?
A) 244
B) 296
C) 488
D) 540

8) A cafeteria serves spaghetti to senior citizens on Fridays. The spaghetti comes prepared in large containers, and each container holds 15 servings of spaghetti. The cafeteria is expecting 82 senior citizens this Friday. What is the least number of containers of spaghetti that the cafeteria will need in order to serve all 82 people?
A) 4
B) 5
C) 6
D) 7

9) A caterpillar travels 10.5 inches in 45 seconds. How far will it travel in 6 minutes?
A) 45 inches
B) 63 inches
C) 64 inches
D) 84 inches

10) Which one of the values will correctly satisfy the following mathematical statement:
$^2/_3 < ? < ^7/_9$

A) $^1/_3$
B) $^1/_5$
C) $^7/_{10}$
D) $^1/_2$

11) Data on the number of vehicles involved in traffic accidents in Cedar Valley on certain dates is represented in the chart below.

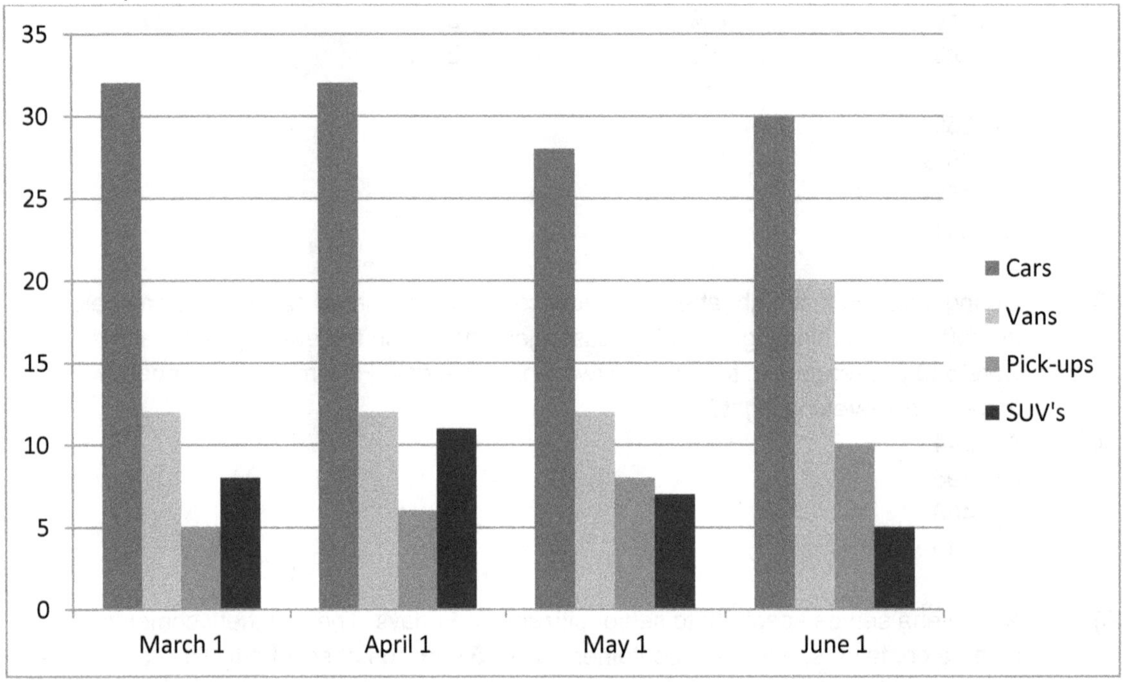

Pick-ups and vans were involved in approximately what percentage of total vehicle accidents on June 1?

A) 50%
B) 46%
C) 40%
D) 31%

12) A company is making its budget for the cost of employees to attend conferences for the year. It costs $7,500 per year in total for the company plus C dollars per employee. During the year, the company has E employees. If the company has budgeted $65,000 for conference attendance, which equation can be used to calculate the maximum cost per employee?

A) ($65,000 – $7,500) ÷ E
B) ($65,000 – $7,500) ÷ C
C) (C – $7,500) ÷ E
D) $65,000 ÷ E

13) The pictograph below illustrates the results of a customer satisfaction survey by region. Each of the four regions has one salesperson. Salespeople in each region receive bonuses based on the amount of positive customer feedback they receive. If the salespeople from all four regions received $540 in bonuses in total, how much bonus money does the company pay each individual salesperson per satisfied customer?

Region 1	
Region 2	
Region 3	
Region 4	

Each  represents positive feedback from 10 customers.

A) $4.00
B) $4.50
C) $4.90
D) $5.00

14) 110 students took a math test. The mean score for the 60 female students was 95, while the mean score for the 50 male students was 90. Which figure below best approximates the mean test score for all 110 students in the class?
A) 55
B) 90
C) 92.5
D) 92.73

15) Carmen wanted to find the mean of the five tests she has taken this semester. However, she erroneously divided the total points from the five tests by 4, which gave her a result of 90. What is the correct mean of her five tests?
A) 72
B) 85
C) 86
D) 95

16) Return on investment (ROI) percentages are provided for seven companies. The ROI will be negative if the company operated at a loss, but the ROI will be a positive value if the company operated at a profit. The ROI's for the seven companies were: –2%, 5%, 7.5%, 14%, 17%, 1.3%, –3%. Which figure below best approximates the mean ROI for the seven companies?
A) 2%
B) 5.7%
C) 6.25%
D) 7.5%

17) In an athletic competition, the maximum possible amount of points was 25 points per participant. The scores for 15 different participants are displayed in the graph below. What was the median score for the 15 participants?

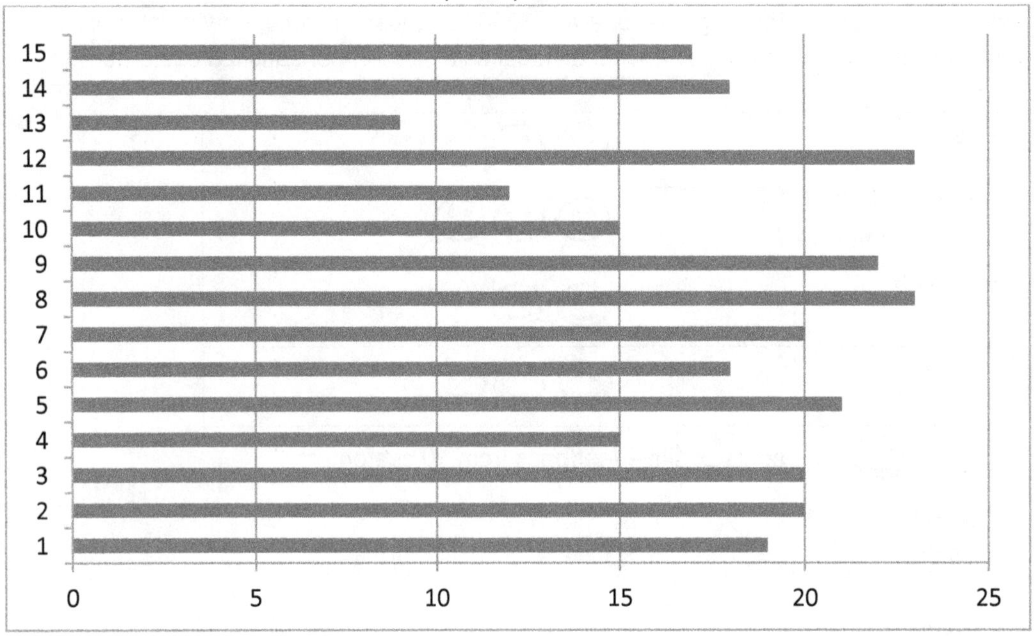

A) 8
B) 15
C) 17
D) 19

Algebra problems:

18) Which of the following is equivalent to the expression $2(x + 2)(x - 3)$ for all values of x?
A) $2x^2 - 2x - 12$
B) $2x^2 - 10x - 6$
C) $2x^2 + 2x - 12$
D) $2x^2 + 10x - 6$

19) A plumber charges $100 per job, plus $25 per hour worked. He is going to do 5 jobs this month. He will earn a total of $4,000. How many hours will he work this month?
A) 10
B) 40
C) 80
D) 140

20) What are two possible values of x for the following equation? $x^2 + 6x + 8 = 0$
A) 1 and 2
B) 2 and 4
C) 6 and 8
D) –2 and –4

21) Factor the following: $2xy - 6x^2y + 4x^2y^2$

A) $2xy(1 + 3x - 2xy)$
B) $2xy(1 - 3x + 2xy)$
C) $2xy(1 + 3x + 2xy)$
D) $2xy(1 - 3x - 2xy)$

22) Which of the following mathematical expressions equals $^3/_{xy}$?

A) $^3/_x \times {}^3/_y$
B) $3 \div 3xy$
C) $3 \div (xy)$
D) $^1/_3 \div 3xy$

23)

$$\frac{x^5}{x^2 - 6x} + \frac{5}{x} = ?$$

A)
$$\frac{x^5 + 5x - 30}{x^2 - 6x}$$

B)
$$\frac{4x^2 - 16x}{x^7}$$

C)
$$\frac{x^5 + 5x + 30}{x^2 - 6x}$$

D)
$$\frac{x^5 + 5x - 30}{x^2 + 6x}$$

24) One-half inch on a map represents M miles. Which of the following equations represents $M + 5$ miles on the map?

A) $\frac{M+5}{2M}$

B) $\frac{0.5M+2.5}{M}$

C) $\frac{2M+5}{M}$

D) $\frac{M+5}{2}$

25) $40 - \frac{3x}{5} \geq 10$, then $x \leq$?

A) 15
B) 30
C) 40
D) 50

26) The number of visitors a museum had on Tuesday (T) was twice as much as the number of visitors it had on Monday (M). The number of visitors it had on Wednesday (W) was 20% greater than that on Tuesday. Which equation can be used to calculate the total number of visitors to the museum for the three days?

A) W + .20W + 2T + M
B) 2M + T + W
C) M + 1.2T + W
D) 5.4M

27) A construction company is building new homes on a housing development. It has an agreement with the municipality that H number of houses must be built every 30 days. If H number of houses are not built during the 30 day period, the company has to pay a penalty to the municipality of P dollars per house. The penalty is paid per house for the number of houses that fall short of the 30-day target. If A represents the actual number of houses built during the 30-day period, which equation below can be used to calculate the penalty for the 30-day period?

A) $(H - P) \times 30$
B) $(H - A) \times P$
C) $(A - H) \times 30$
D) $(A - H) \times P$

28) Simplify: $\sqrt{7} + 2\sqrt{7}$

A) 14
B) $3\sqrt{7}$
C) $2\sqrt{14}$
D) $3\sqrt{14}$

29) $(x^2 - x - 12) \div (x - 4) = ?$

A) $(x + 3)$
B) $(x - 3)$
C) $(-x + 3)$
D) $(-x - 3)$

30) If $x - 1 > 0$ and $y = x - 1$, then $y > ?$

A) x
B) $x + 1$
C) $x - 1$
D) 0

31) If $5 + 5(3\sqrt{x} + 4) = 55$, then $\sqrt{x} = ?$

A) –4
B) –2
C) 2
D) 4

Geometry and graphing problems:

32) State the x and y intercepts that fall on the straight line represented by the following equation:
$y = x + 6$

A) (–6,0) and (0,6)
B) (0,6) and (0,–6)
C) (6,0) and (0,–6)
D) (0,–6) and (6,0)

33) Find the coordinates (x, y) of the midpoint of the line segment on a graph that connects the points (–5, 3) and (3, –5).

A) (–1,–1)
B) (–1,1)
C) (1,–1)
D) (1,1)

34) Consider a two-dimensional linear graph where $x = 3$ and $y = 14$. The line crosses the y axis at 5. What is the slope of this line?

A) 2.2 B) 3.0 C) 6.33 D) –2.2

35) For the two functions $f_1(x)$ and $f_2(x)$, tables of values are given below. What is the value of $f_2(f_1(2))$?

x	$f_1(x)$
1	3
2	5
3	7
4	9
5	11

x	$f_2(x)$
2	4
3	9
4	16
5	25
6	36

A) 4 B) 5 C) 9 D) 25

36) The graph below shows the relationship between the number of days of rain per month and the amount of people who exercise outdoors per month. What relationship can be observed?

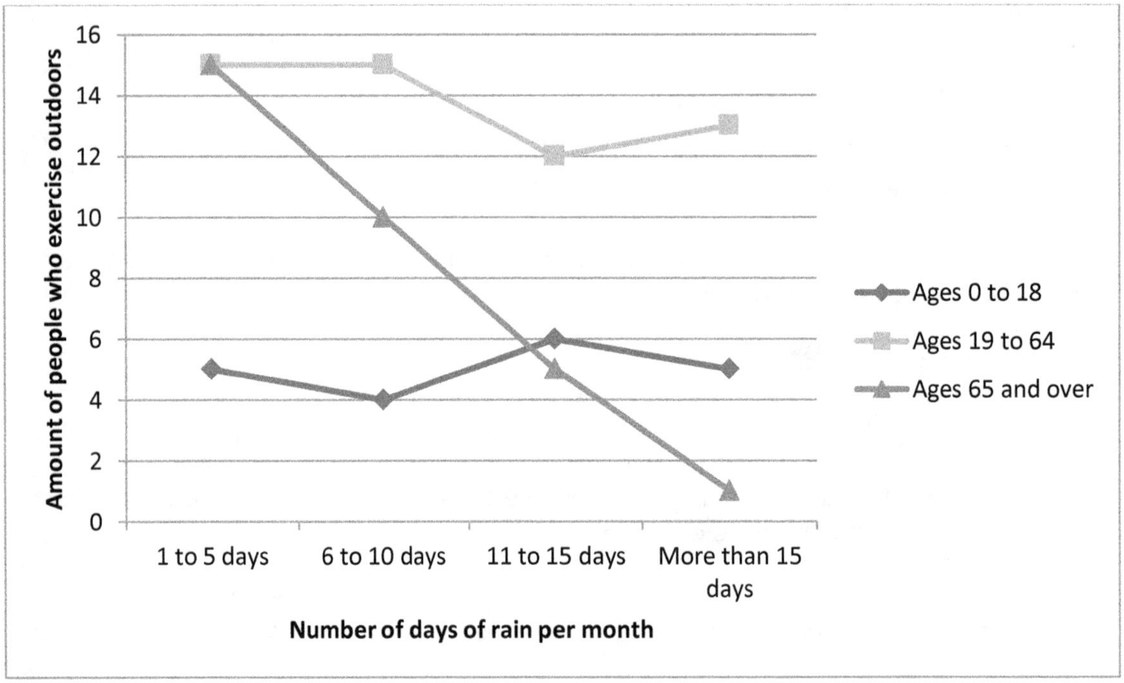

A) Young children are reliant upon an adult in order to exercise outdoors.
B) The exercise habits of working age people seem to fluctuate proportionately to the amount of rainfall.
C) In the 19 to 64 age group, there is a negative relationship between the number of days of rain and the amount of people who exercise outdoors.
D) People aged 65 and over seem less inclined to exercise outdoors when there is more rain.

37) Consider the scatterplot below and then choose the best answer from the options that follow.

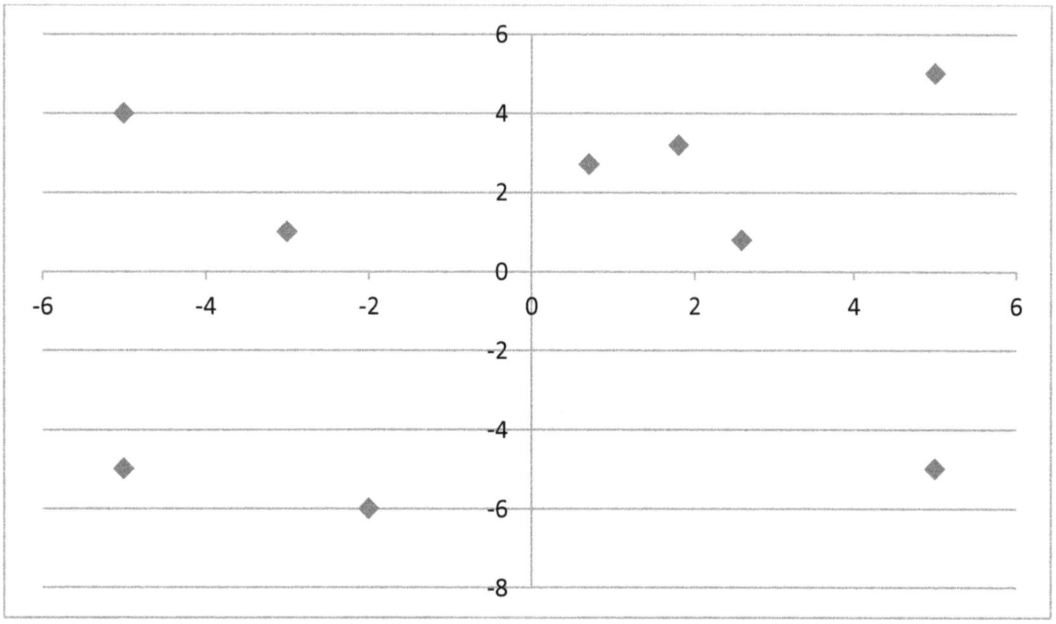

A) The scatterplot suggests a strong positive linear relationship between x and y.

B) The scatterplot suggests a strong negative linear relationship between x and y.

C) The scatterplot suggests that there is no relationship between x and y.

D) The scatterplot suggests a weak negative linear relationship between x and y.

38) The graph of a line is shown on the xy plane below. The point that has the y-coordinate of 45 is not shown. What is the corresponding x-coordinate of that point?

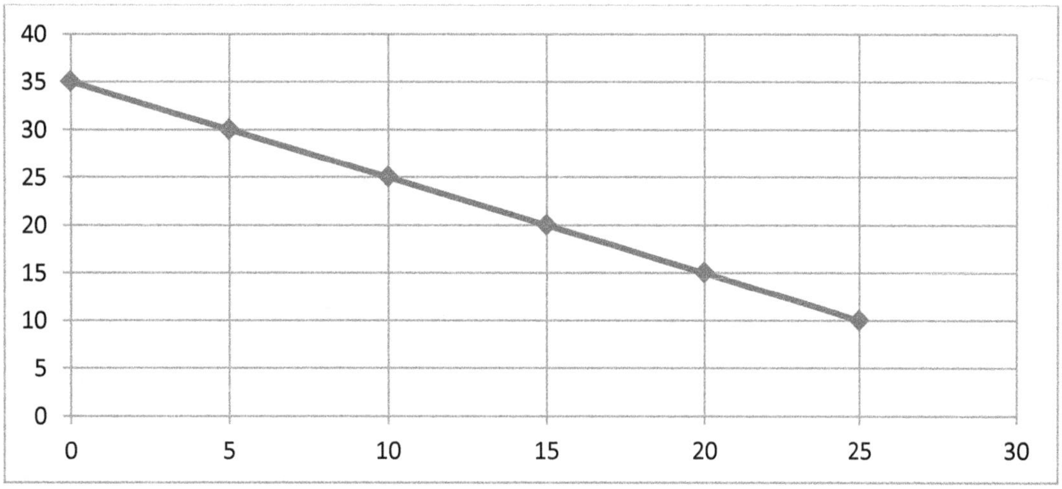

A) –10
B) –5
C) 0
D) 5

39) The graph of a line is shown on the *xy* plane below. The point that has the *x*-coordinate of 160 is not shown. What is the corresponding *y*-coordinate of that point?

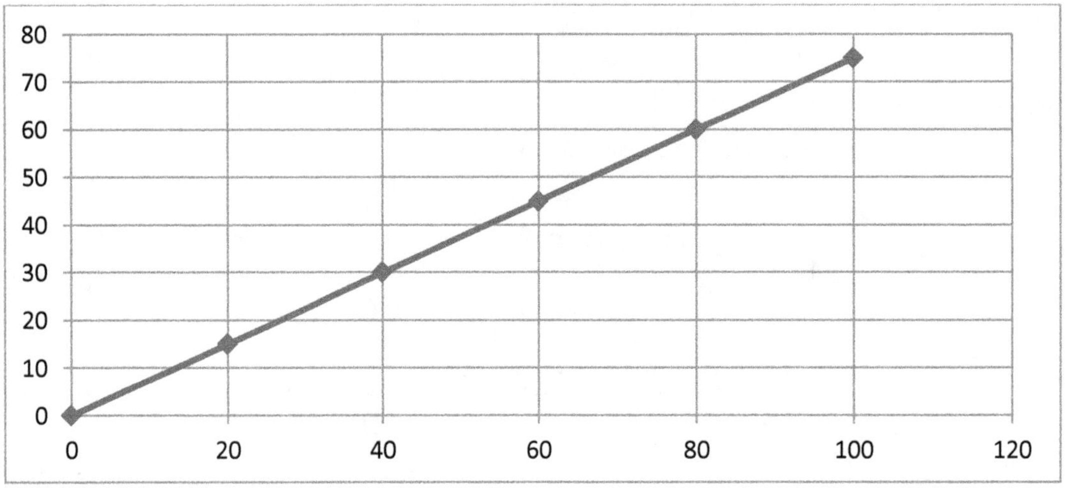

A) 115
B) 120
C) 125
D) 130

40) The central angle in the circle below measures 60° and is subtended by arc A which is 7π centimeters in length. How many centimeters long is the radius of this circle?

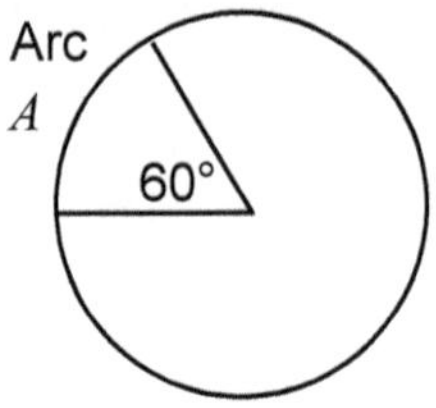

A) 42
B) 21
C) 6π
D) 6

41) In the figure below, ∠Y is a right angle and ∠X = 60°.

If line segment YZ is 5 units long, then how long is line segment XY?

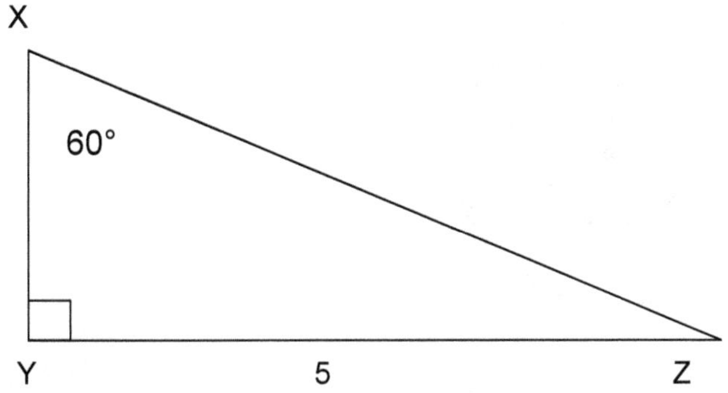

A) $5/\sqrt{3}$ units
B) 5 units
C) 6 units
D) 15 units

42) The figure in the *xy* plane below is going to be moved 7 units to the right and 6 units down. What will the coordinates of point C be after the shift?

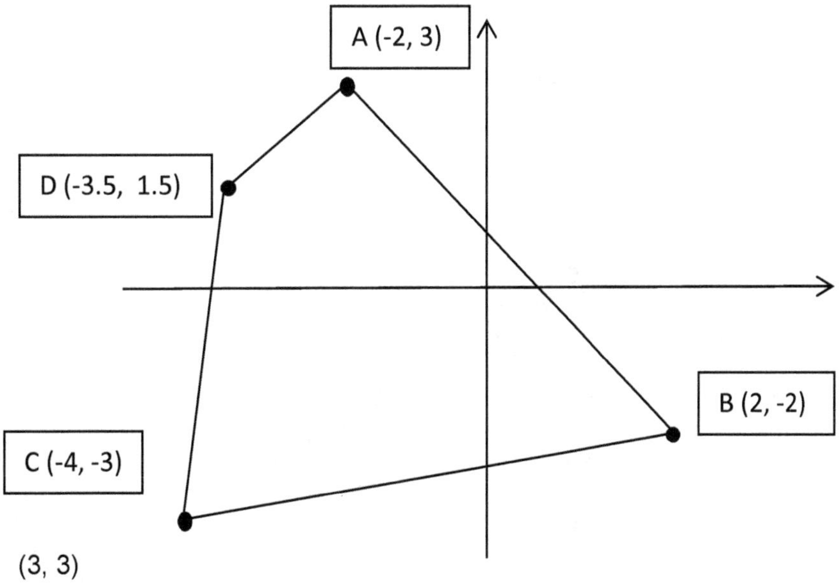

A) (3, 3)
B) (9, –8)
C) (3, –9)
D) (–11, –9)

43) Consider two concentric circles with radii of $R_1 = 1$ and $R_2 = 2.4$ as shown in the illustration below. Line L forms the diameter of the circles. What is the area of the lined part of the illustration?

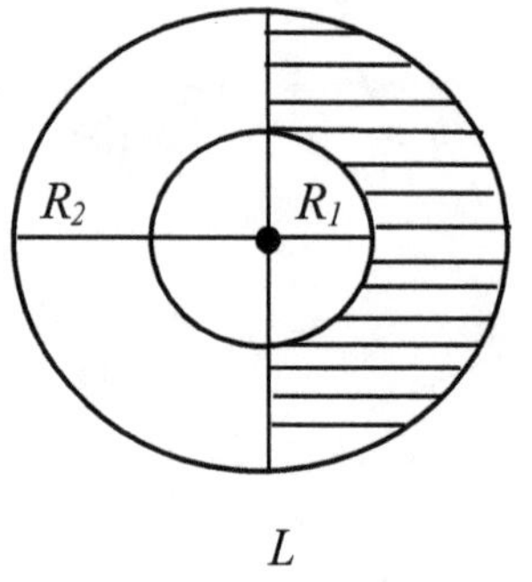

A) 0.7π
B) 1.4π
C) 2π
D) 2.38π

44) The line on the xy-graph below forms the diameter of the circle. What is the approximate circumference of the circle?

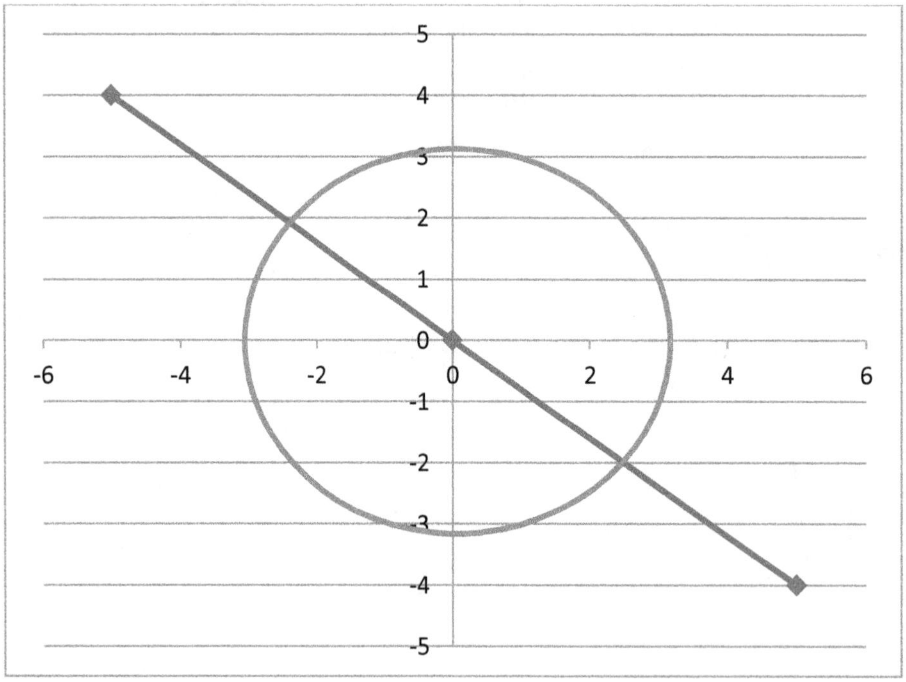

A) 3π
B) 6
C) 6π
D) 9

45) Mr. Lee is going to build a new garage. The garage will have a square base and a pyramid-shaped roof. The base measurement of the house is 20 feet. The height of the interior of the garage is 18 feet. The height of the roof from the center of its base to its peak is 15 feet. A diagram of the garage is shown below:

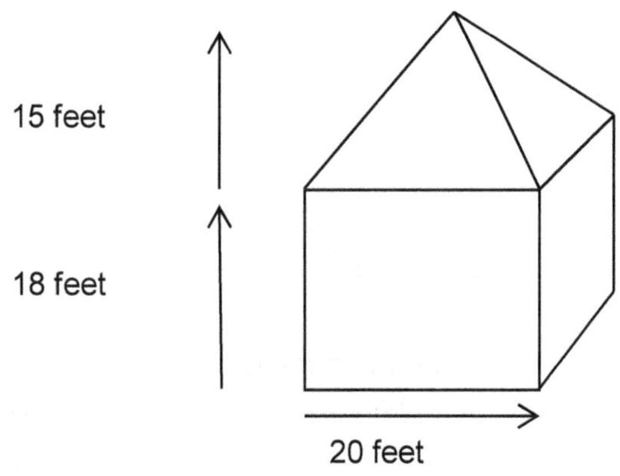

What fraction expresses the ratio of the volume of the roof of the garage to the volume of the interior of the garage?

A) $^{5}/_{6}$

B) $^{5}/_{18}$

C) $^{1}/_{4}$

D) $^{3}/_{4}$

46) Which of the following statements about parallelograms is true?
A) A parallelogram has no right angles.
B) A parallelogram has opposite angles which are congruent.
C) A parallelogram has only one pair of parallel sides.
D) A rhombus cannot be classified as a parallelogram.

47) Which of the following statements best describes supplementary angles?
A) Supplementary angles must add up to 90 degrees.
B) Supplementary angles must add up to 180 degrees.
C) Supplementary angles must add up to 360 degrees.
D) Supplementary angles must be congruent angles.

48) The area of a rectangle is 168 square units. This rectangle contains smaller rectangles that measure 2 square units each. How many of these small rectangles are needed to make up the entire rectangle?
A) 13
B) 28
C) 42
D) 84

49) Acme Packaging uses string to secure their packages prior to shipment. The string is tied around the entire length and entire width of the package, as shown in the following illustration:

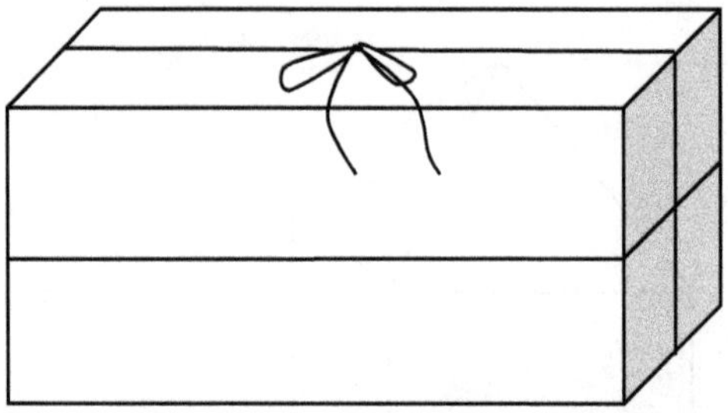

The box is ten inches in height, ten inches in depth, and twenty inches in length. An additional fifteen inches of string is needed to tie a bow on the top of the package. How much string is needed in total in order to tie up the entire package, including making the bow on the top?

A) 135
B) 120
C) 100
D) 80

50) The triangle in the illustration below is an equilateral triangle. What is the measurement in degrees of angle a?

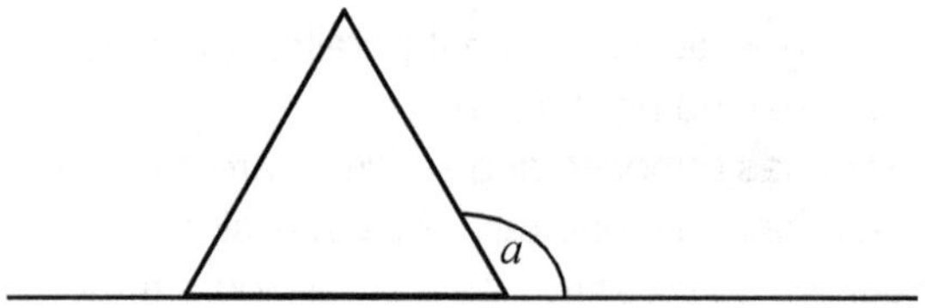

A) 40
B) 45
C) 60
D) 120

TABE Practice Math Test 3 – Answer Key

1) A
2) C
3) A
4) A
5) D
6) B
7) A
8) C
9) D
10) C
11) B
12) A
13) B
14) D
15) A
16) B
17) D
18) A
19) D
20) D
21) B
22) C
23) A
24) B
25) D
26) D
27) B
28) B
29) A
30) D
31) C
32) A
33) A
34) B
35) D

36) D

37) C

38) A

39) B

40) B

41) A

42) C

43) D

44) C

45) B

46) B

47) B

48) D

49) A

50) D

TABE Practice Math Test 3 – Solutions and Explanations

1) The correct answer is A. For problems with decimals, line the figures up in a column and add zeroes to fill in the column as shown below:

0.5400
0.0540
0.0450
0.5045

If you still struggle with decimals, you can remove the decimal points and the zeroes before the other integers in order to see the answer more clearly.

~~0.~~5400
~~0.0~~540
~~0.0~~450
~~0.~~5045
~~0.00~~54

When we have removed the zeroes in front of the other numbers, we can see that the largest number is the first one, which is 0.54.

2) The correct answer is C. Each panel is 8 feet 6 inches long, and he needs 11 panels to cover the entire side of the field. So, we need to multiply 8 feet 6 inches by 11, and then simplify the result. Step 1: 8 feet × 11 = 88 feet; Step 2: 6 inches × 11 = 66 inches; Step 3: There are 12 inches in a foot, so we need to determine how many feet and inches there are in 66 inches. 66 inches ÷ 12 = 5 feet 6 inches; Step 4: Now add the two results together. 88 feet + 5 feet 6 inches = 93 feet 6 inches

3) The correct answer is A. This problem is like question 1 above, except here we need to find a missing value. Remember to put in zeroes and line up the decimal points when you compare the numbers.

0.0007
A. 0.0012
B. 0.0006
C. 0.0022
D. 0.0220
0.0021

Answer choice B is less than 0.0007, and answer choices C and D are greater than 0.0021. Answer choice A (0.0012) is between 0.0007 and 0.0021, so it is the correct answer.

4) The correct answer is A. The equation is: F = \$500P + \$3,700. We are told that the total funds are \$40,000 so put that in the equation to solve the problem.
\$40,000 = \$500P + \$3,700
\$40,000 – \$3,700 = \$500P
\$36,300 = \$500P
\$36,300 ÷ 500 = \$500 ÷ 500P

$36,300 ÷ 500 = 72.6
Since a fraction of a project cannot be undertaken, the greatest number of projects is 72.

5) The correct answer is D. To answer this type of question, you need these principles: (a) Positive numbers are greater than negative numbers; (b) When two fractions have the same numerator, the fraction with the smaller number in the denominator is the larger fraction. Accordingly, 1 is greater than $^1/_5$; $^1/_5$ is greater than $^1/_7$, and $^1/_7$ is greater than $-^1/_3$.

6) The correct answer is B. The dark gray part at the bottom of each bar represents those students who will attend the dance. 45% of the freshman, 30% of the sophomores, 38% of the juniors, and 30% of the seniors will attend. Calculating the average, we get the overall percentage for all four grades: (45 + 30 + 38 + 30) ÷ 4 = 35.75%. 35% is the closest answer to 35.75%, so it best approximates our result.

7) The correct answer is A. The problem tells us that the morning flight had 52 passengers more than the evening flight, and there were 540 passengers in total on the two flights that day. Step 1: First of all, we need to deduct the difference from the total: 540 – 52 = 488; In other words, there were 488 passengers on both flights combined, plus the 52 additional passengers on the morning flight. Step 2: Now divide this result by 2 to allocate an amount of passengers to each flight: 488 ÷ 2 = 244 passengers on the evening flight. (Had the question asked you for the amount of passengers on the morning flight, you would have had to add back the amount of additional passengers to find the total amount of passengers for the morning flight:
244 + 52 = 296 passengers on the morning flight)

8) The correct answer is C. Divide and then round up: 82 people in total ÷ 15 people served per container = 5.467 containers. We need to round up to 6 since we cannot purchase a fractional part of a container.

9) The correct answer is D. The question is asking us about a time duration of 6 minutes, so we need to calculate the amount of seconds in 6 minutes: 6 minutes × 60 seconds per minute = 360 seconds in total. Then divide the total time by the amount of time needed to make one journey: 360 seconds ÷ 45 seconds per journey = 8 journeys. Finally, multiply the number of journeys by the amount of inches per journey in order to get the total inches: 10.5 inches for 1 journey × 8 journeys = 84 inches in total

10) The correct answer is C. First of all, we need to find a common denominator for the fractions in the inequality, as well as for the fractions in the answer choices. In order to complete the problem quickly, you should not try to find the lowest common denominator, but just find any common denominator. We can do this by expressing all of the numbers with a denominator of 90, since 9 is the largest denominator in the inequality and 10 is the largest denominator in the answer choices.

$^2/_3 \times {}^{30}/_{30} = {}^{60}/_{90}$
$^7/_9 \times {}^{10}/_{10} = {}^{70}/_{90}$

Then, express the original inequality in terms of the common denominator: $^{60}/_{90} < ? < {}^{70}/_{90}$

Next, convert the answer choices to the common denominator.

A. $^{1}/_{3} \times ^{30}/_{30} = ^{30}/_{90}$
B. $^{1}/_{5} \times ^{18}/_{18} = ^{18}/_{90}$
C. $^{7}/_{10} \times ^{9}/_{9} = ^{63}/_{90}$
D. $^{1}/_{2} \times ^{45}/_{45} = ^{45}/_{90}$

Finally, compare the results to find the answer. By comparing the numerators (the top numbers of the fractions), we can see that $^{63}/_{90}$ lies between $^{60}/_{90}$ and $^{70}/_{90}$. So, C is the correct answer because $^{60}/_{90} < ^{63}/_{90} < ^{70}/_{90}$.

11) The correct answer is B. In this question, we have an example of a histogram. Histograms are like bar graphs except they show data for groups. To answer these types of questions, be sure that you get the data from the correct group or groups. Here, we need to look at the bars for June 1 at the far right side of the graph. First, find the total amount of accidents on that date. Cars were involved in 30 accidents, vans in 20 accidents, pick-ups in 10 accidents, and SUV's in 5 accidents. So, there were 65 accidents in total (30 + 20 + 10 + 5 = 65). Then divide the number of accidents for pick-ups and vans into the total: 30 ÷ 65 = 46.1538% ≈ 46%

12) The correct answer is A. The total amount of the budget is \$65,000. The up-front cost is \$7,500, so we can determine the remaining amount of available funds by deducting the up-front cost from the total: \$65,000 – \$7,500. We have to divide the available amount by the number of employees (E) to get the maximum cost per employee: (\$65,000 – \$7,500) ÷ E

13) The correct answer is B. First of all, add up the amount of faces on the chart: 4 + 3 + 2 + 3 = 12 faces. Each face represents 10 customers, so multiply to get the total number of customers: 12 × 10 = 120 customers in total for all four regions. The salespeople received \$540 in total, so we need to divide this by the amount of customers: \$540 ÷ 120 customers = \$4.50 per customer

14) The correct answer is D. You need to find the total points for all the females and the total points for all the males: Females: 60 × 95 = 5700; Males: 50 × 90 = 4500. Then add these two amounts together and divide by the total number of students in the class to get your solution: (5700 + 4500) ÷ 110 = 10,200 ÷ 110 = 92.73 average for all 110 students

15) The correct answer is A. First you need to find the total points that the student earned. You do this by taking Carmen's erroneous average times 4: 4 × 90 = 360. Then divide the total points earned by the correct number of tests in order to get the correct average: 360 ÷ 5 = 72

16) The correct answer is B. The mean is the arithmetic average. First, add up all of the items: –2% + 5% + 7.5% + 14% + 17% + 1.3% + –3% = 39.8%. Then divide by 7 since there are 7 companies in the set: 39.8% ÷ 7 = 5.68% ≈ 5.7%

17) The correct answer is D. The median is the number that is halfway through the set. Our data set is: 19, 20, 20, 15, 21, 18, 20, 23, 22, 15, 12, 23, 9, 18, 17. First, put the numbers in ascending order: 9, 12, 15, 15, 17, 18, 18, 19, 20, 20, 20, 21, 22, 23, 23. We have 15 numbers, so the 8th number in the set is halfway and is therefore the median:
9, 12, 15, 15, 17, 18, 18, **19**, 20, 20, 20, 21, 22, 23, 23

18) The correct answer is A. The FOIL method is used on polynomials, which are equations that look like this: $(a + b)(c + d)$

You multiply the variables or terms in the parentheses in this order:
First **I**nside **O**utside **L**ast

We can use the FOIL method on our example equation as follows:
$(a + b)(c + d) =$
$(a \times c) + (a \times d) + (b \times c) + (b \times d) =$
$ac + ad + bc + bd$

You should use the FOIL method in this problem. Be very careful with the negative numbers when doing the multiplication.
$2(x + 2)(x - 3) =$
$2[(x \times x) + (x \times -3) + (2 \times x) + (2 \times -3)] =$
$2(x^2 + -3x + 2x + -6) =$
$2(x^2 - 3x + 2x - 6) =$
$2(x^2 - x - 6)$

Then multiply each term by the 2 at the front of the parentheses.
$2(x^2 - x - 6) =$
$2x^2 - 2x - 12$

19) The correct answer is D. The plumber is going to earn $4,000 for the month. He charges a set fee of $100 per job, and he will do 5 jobs, so we can calculate the total set fees first: $100 set fee per job × 5 jobs = $500 total set fees. Then deduct the set fees from the total for the month in order to determine the total for the hourly pay: $4,000 – $500 = $3,500. He earns $25 per hour, so divide the hourly rate into the total hourly pay in order to determine the number of hours he will work: $3,500 total hourly pay ÷ $25 per hour = 140 hours to work

20) The correct answer is D.

Step 1: Factor the equation.
$x^2 + 6x + 8 = 0$
$(x + 2)(x + 4) = 0$

Step 2: Now substitute 0 for x in the first pair of parentheses.
$(0 + 2)(x + 4) = 0$
$2(x + 4) = 0$
$2x + 8 = 0$
$2x + 8 - 8 = 0 - 8$
$2x = -8$
$2x \div 2 = -8 \div 2$
$x = -4$

Step 3: Then substitute 0 for x in the second pair of parentheses.
$(x + 2)(x + 4) = 0$
$(x + 2)(0 + 4) = 0$
$(x + 2)4 = 0$
$4x + 8 = 0$
$4x + 8 - 8 = 0 - 8$

$4x = -8$
$4x \div 4 = -8 \div 4$
$x = -2$

21) The correct answer is B. Looking at this equation, we can see that each term contains x. We can also see that each term contains y. So, first factor out xy.
$2xy - 6x^2y + 4x^2y^2 =$
$xy(2 - 6x + 4xy)$

Then, think about integers. We can see that all of the terms inside the parentheses are divisible by 2. Now let's factor out the 2. To do this, we divide each term inside the parentheses by 2.
$xy(2 - 6x + 4xy) =$
$2xy(1 - 3x + 2xy)$

22) The correct answer is C. The line in a fraction is the same as the division symbol. For example, $^a/_b = a \div b$. In the same way, $^3/_{xy} = 3 \div (xy)$.

23) The correct answer is A. Find the lowest common denominator. Since x is common to both denominators, we can convert the denominator of the second fraction to the LCD by multiplying by $(x - 6)$.

$$\frac{x^5}{x^2 - 6x} + \frac{5}{x} =$$

$$\frac{x^5}{x^2 - 6x} + \left(\frac{5}{x} \times \frac{x-6}{x-6}\right) =$$

$$\frac{x^5}{x^2 - 6x} + \frac{5x - 30}{x^2 - 6x} =$$

$$\frac{x^5 + 5x - 30}{x^2 - 6x}$$

24) The correct answer is B. The ratio of 0.5 inch for M miles can be represented mathematically as $\frac{0.5}{M}$. The ratio for $M + 5$ is not known, so we can represent the unknown as x: $\frac{x}{M+5}$. Finally, use cross multiplication to solve the problem:

$$\frac{0.5}{M} = \frac{x}{M+5}$$

$0.5 \times (M + 5) = Mx$

Then divide by M to isolate x and solve the problem.

$[0.5 \times (M + 5)] \div M = Mx \div M$

$$\frac{0.5M + 2.5}{M} = x$$

25) The correct answer is D. Deal with the whole numbers on each side of the inequality first.

$$40 - \frac{3x}{5} \geq 10$$

$$(40 - 40) - \frac{3x}{5} \geq 10 - 40$$

$$-\frac{3x}{5} \geq -30$$

Then deal with the fraction.

$$-\frac{3x}{5} \geq -30$$

$$\left(5 \times -\frac{3x}{5}\right) \geq -30 \times 5$$

$$-3x \geq -30 \times 5$$
$$-3x \geq -150$$

Then deal with the remaining whole numbers.

$$-3x \geq -150$$
$$-3x \div 3 \geq -150 \div 3$$
$$-x \geq -150 \div 3$$
$$-x \geq -50$$

Then deal with the negative number.

$$-x \geq -50$$
$$-x + 50 \geq -50 + 50$$
$$-x + 50 \geq 0$$

Finally, isolate the unknown variable as a positive number.

$$-x + 50 \geq 0$$
$$-x + x + 50 \geq 0 + x$$
$$50 \geq x$$
$$x \leq 50$$

26) The correct answer is D. Set up each part of the problem as an equation. The museum had twice as many visitors on Tuesday (T) as on Monday (M), so T = 2M. The number of visitors on Wednesday exceeded that of Tuesday by 20%, so W = 1.20 × T. Then express T in terms of M for Wednesday's visitors: W = 1.20 × T = 1.20 × 2M = 2.40M. Finally, add the amounts together for all three days: M + 2M + 2.40M = 5.4M

27) The correct answer is B. First, we need to calculate the shortage in the amount of houses actually built. If H represents the amount of houses that should be built and A represents the actual number of houses built, then the shortage is calculated as: $H - A$. The company has to pay

P dollars per house for the shortage, so we calculate the total penalty by multiplying the shortage by the penalty per house: $(H - A) \times P$

28) The correct answer is B. In order to add square roots like this, you need to add the numbers in front of the square root sign. If there is no number before the radical, then put in the number 1 because the radical will count only 1 time in that case.

$\sqrt{7} + 2\sqrt{7} =$

$1\sqrt{7} + 2\sqrt{7} =$

$3\sqrt{7}$

29) The correct answer is A. In order to solve the problem, you have to do long division of the quadratic.

$$\begin{array}{r} x + 3 \\ x - 4\overline{)x^2 - x - 12} \\ \underline{x^2 - 4x} \\ 3x - 12 \\ \underline{3x - 12} \\ 0 \end{array}$$

30) The correct answer is D. Notice that both the inequality and the equation contain $x - 1$. Since the equation has the equals sign, we can just substitute y for $x - 1$ in the inequality.

$x - 1 > 0$

$x - 1 = y$

$y > 0$

31) The correct answer is C. First, deal with the integers that are outside the parentheses.

$5 + 5(3\sqrt{x} + 4) = 55$

$5 + 15\sqrt{x} + 20 = 55$

$25 + 15\sqrt{x} = 55$

$25 - 25 + 15\sqrt{x} = 55 - 25$

$15\sqrt{x} = 30$

Then divide in order to isolate $\sqrt{x}$.

$15\sqrt{x} = 30$

$(15\sqrt{x}) \div 15 = 30 \div 15$

$\sqrt{x} = 2$

32) The correct answer is A. Remember that the y intercept exists where the line crosses the y axis, so $x = 0$ for the y intercept. Begin by substituting 0 for x.

$y = x + 6$

$y = 0 + 6$

$y = 6$

Therefore, the coordinates (0, 6) represent the y intercept.
On the other hand, the x intercept exists where the line crosses the x axis, so $y = 0$ for the x intercept. Now substitute 0 for y.

$y = x + 6$

$0 = x + 6$

$0 - 6 = x + 6 - 6$

$-6 = x$

So, the coordinates (–6, 0) represent the x intercept.

33) The correct answer is A. Remember that in order to find midpoints on a line, you need to use the midpoint formula. For two points on a graph (x_1, y_1) and (x_2, y_2), the midpoint is:

$(x_1 + x_2) \div 2$, $(y_1 + y_2) \div 2$

$(-5 + 3) \div 2 =$ midpoint x, $(3 + -5) \div 2 =$ midpoint y

$-2 \div 2 =$ midpoint x, $-2 \div 2 =$ midpoint y

$-1 =$ midpoint x, $-1 =$ midpoint y

34) The correct answer is B. When you are provided with a set of coordinates and the y intercept, you need the slope-intercept formula in order to calculate the slope of a line.
In the slope-intercept formula, m is the slope and b is the y intercept, which is the point where the line crosses the y axis. Now solve for the numbers given in the problem.

$y = mx + b$

$14 = m3 + 5$

$14 - 5 = m3 + 5 - 5$

$9 = m3$

$9 \div 3 = m$

$3 = m$

35) The correct answer is D. First, solve for the function in the inner–most set of parentheses, in this case $f_1(x)$. For $x = 2$, $f_1(2) = 5$

Then, take this new value to solve for $f_2(x)$. For $x = 5$, $f_2(x) = 25$

36) The correct answer is D. The most striking relationship on the graph is the line for ages 65 and over, which clearly shows a negative relationship between exercising outdoors and the number of days of rain per month. You will recall that a negative relationship exists when an increase in one variable causes a decrease in the other variable. So, we can conclude that people aged 65 and over seem less inclined to exercise outdoors when there is more rain.

37) The correct answer is C. When looking at scatterplots, try to see if the dots are roughly grouped into any kind of pattern or line. If so, positive or negative relationships may be represented. Here, however, the dots are located at what appear to be random places on all four quadrants of the graph. So, the scatterplot suggests that there is no relationship between x and y.

38) The correct answer is A. As x decreases by 5, y increases by 5. So, if we want to determine the x coordinate for (x, 45) we need to deduct 10 from the x coordinate of (0, 35). Therefore, the coordinates are (–10, 45), and the answer is –10.

39) The correct answer is B. We can see that when $x = 80$, $y = 60$. So, when $x = 160$, $y = 120$. Alternatively, you can determine that the line represents the function: $f(x) = x \times 0.75$. Then substitute 160 for x: $x \times 0.75 = 160 \times 0.75 = 120$

40) The correct answer is B. Use the formula for circumference: $\pi \times$ radius $\times$ 2. The angle given in the problem is 60°. If we divide the total 360° in the circle by the 60° angle, we determine that: 360 ÷ 60 = 6. So, there are 6 such arcs along this circle. We then have to multiply the number of arcs by the length of each arc to get the circumference of the circle: $6 \times 7\pi = 42\pi$. Then, use the formula for the circumference of the circle to solve.

$42\pi = \pi \times 2 \times$ radius
$42\pi \div 2 = \pi \times 2 \times$ radius $\div 2$
$21\pi = \pi \times$ radius
21 = radius

41) The correct answer is A. Triangle XYZ is a 30° - 60° - 90° triangle. As a result of the Pythagorean Theorem, we know that its sides are in the ratio of 1: $\sqrt{3}$: 2. In other words, using relative measurements, the line segment opposite the 30° angle is 1 unit long, the line segment opposite the 60° angle is $\sqrt{3}$ units long, and the line segment opposite the right angle (the hypotenuse) is 2 units long. In this problem, line segment XY is opposite the 30° angle, so it is 1 proportional unit long. Line segment YZ is opposite the 60° angle, so it is $\sqrt{3}$ proportional units long. Line segment XZ (the hypotenuse) is the line opposite the right angle, so it is 2 proportional units long. So, in order to keep the measurements in proportion, we need to set up the following proportion: $XY/YZ = 1/\sqrt{3}$

Now substitute the known measurement of YZ from the above figure, which is 5 in this problem.

$$XY/YZ = 1/\sqrt{3}$$
$$(XY/5) = 1/\sqrt{3}$$
$$(XY/5 \times 5) = (1/\sqrt{3} \times 5)$$
$$XY = 5/\sqrt{3}$$

42) The correct answer is C. Before we shift the figure, point C has the coordinates (–4, –3). We are moving the figure 7 units to the right, thereby adding 7 to the x coordinate, and 6 units down, thereby subtracting 6 from the y coordinate. –4 + 7 = 3 and –3 – 6 = –9, so the new coordinates are: (3, –9).

43) The correct answer is D. The formula for the area of a circle is: $\pi \times R^2$. First, we need to calculate the area of the larger circle: $\pi \times 2.4^2 = 5.76\pi$. Then calculate the area of the smaller inner circle: $\pi \times 1^2 = \pi$. We need to find the difference between half of each circle, so divide the area of each circle by 2 and then subtract.

$$(5.76\pi \div 2) - (\pi \div 2) = \frac{5.76\pi}{2} - \frac{\pi}{2} = \frac{4.76\pi}{2} = 2.38\pi$$

44) The correct answer is C. The formula for circumference is: $\pi \times 2 \times R$. The center of the circle is on (0, 0) and the top edge of the circle extends to (0, 3), so the radius of the circle is 3. Therefore, the circumference is: $\pi \times 2 \times 3 = 6\pi$

45) The correct answer is B. The base of the garage is square, so its volume is calculated by taking the length times the width times the height: $20 \times 20 \times 18 = 7200$. The roof of the garage is a pyramid shape, so its volume is calculated by taking one-third of the base squared times the height: $(20 \times 20 \times 15) \times {}^{1}/_{3} = 6000 \div 3 = 2000$. So, the volume of the roof to the interior is: $\frac{2000}{7200} = \frac{5}{18}$

46) The correct answer is B. A parallelogram is a four-sided figure that has two pairs of parallel sides. The opposite or facing sides of a parallelogram are of equal length and the opposite angles of a parallelogram are of equal measure. You will recall that congruent is another word for equal in measure. So, answer B is correct. A rectangle is a parallelogram with four angles of equal size (all of which are right angles), while a square is a parallelogram with four sides of equal length and four right angles. A rhombus looks like a diamond. All of its sides have equal length, its opposite sides are parallel, and its opposite angles are equal. So a rhombus is a parallelogram.

47) The correct answer is B. Two angles are supplementary if they add up to 180 degrees.

48) The correct answer is D. A rectangle consisting of 2 square units will look like the following illustration: 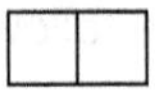

So, we divide the total number of squares in the larger rectangle by 2: 168 ÷ 2 = 84

49) The correct answer is A. The string that goes around the front, back, and sides of the package is calculated as follows: 20 + 10 + 20 + 10 = 60. The string that goes around the top, bottom, and sides of the package is calculated in the same way since the top and bottom are equal in length to the front and back: 20 + 10 + 20 + 10 = 60. So, 120 inches of string is needed so far. Then, we need 15 extra inches for the bow: 120 + 15 = 135

50) The correct answer is D. An equilateral triangle has three equal sides and three equal angles. Since all 3 angles in any triangle need to add up to 180 degrees, each angle of an equilateral triangle is 60 degrees (180 ÷ 3 = 60). Angles that lie along the same side of a straight line must add up to 180. So, we calculate angle a as follows: 180 – 60 = 120

TABE Practice Math Test 4

Number and data problems:

1) Which of the following shows the numbers ordered from least to greatest?

A) 0.2135
0.3152
0.0253
0.0012

B) 0.3152
0.2135
0.0253
0.0012

C) 0.0253
0.0012
0.3152
0.2135

D) 0.0012
0.0253
0.2135
0.3152

2) If $\frac{x}{24}$ is between 8 and 9, which of the following could be the value of x?

A) 190
B) 191
C) 200
D) 217

3) The ratio of bags of apples to bags of oranges in a particular grocery store is 2 to 3. If there are 44 bags of apples in the store, how many bags of oranges are there?

A) 66
B) 55
C) 48
D) 33

4) At the beginning of class, $^1/_5$ of the students leave to go to singing lessons. Then $^1/_4$ of the remaining students leave to go to the principal's office. If 18 students are then left in the class, how many students were there at the beginning of class?

A) 90
B) 45
C) 30
D) 25

5) A dance academy had 300 students at the beginning of January. It lost 5% of its students during the month. However, 15 new students joined the academy on the last day of the month. If this pattern continues for the next two months, how many students will there be at the academy at the end of March?
A) 285
B) 300
C) 310
D) 315

6) In a group of children, one-half have had a tetanus shot. Of that half, only one-third suffered wounds that would have caused tetanus. In which of the following graphs does the dark gray area represent that third of the group?

A)

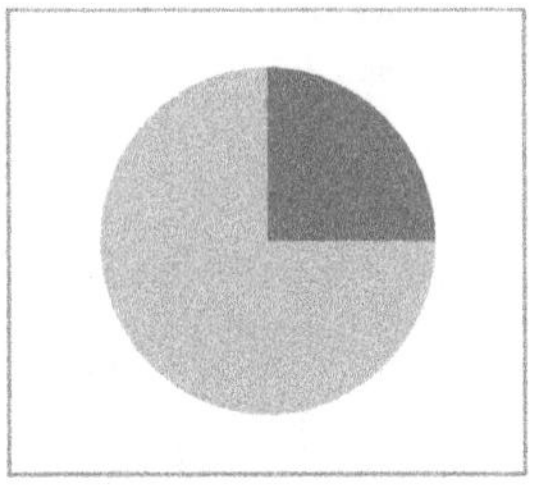

B)

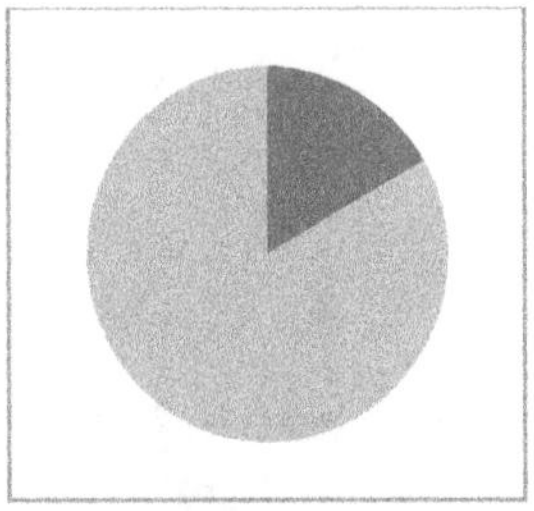

C)

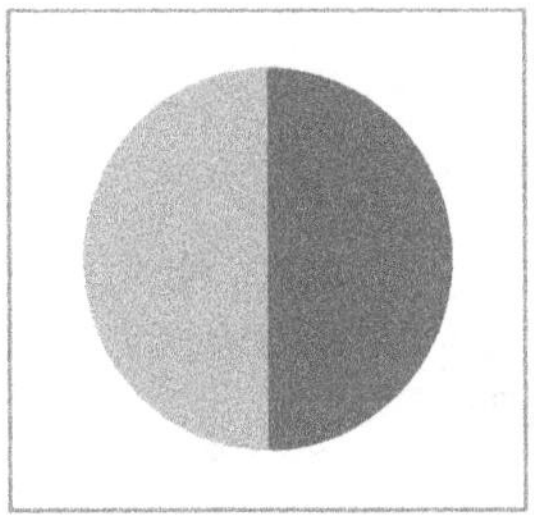

D)

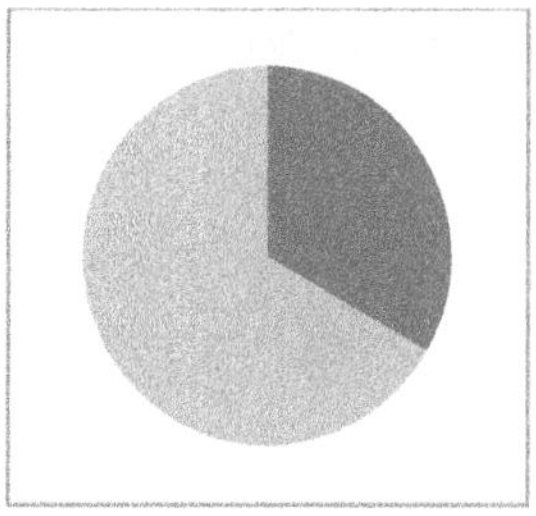

7) The residents of Hendersonville took a census. As part of the census, each resident had to indicate how many relatives they had living within a ten-mile radius of the town. The results of that particular question on the census are represented in the graph below.

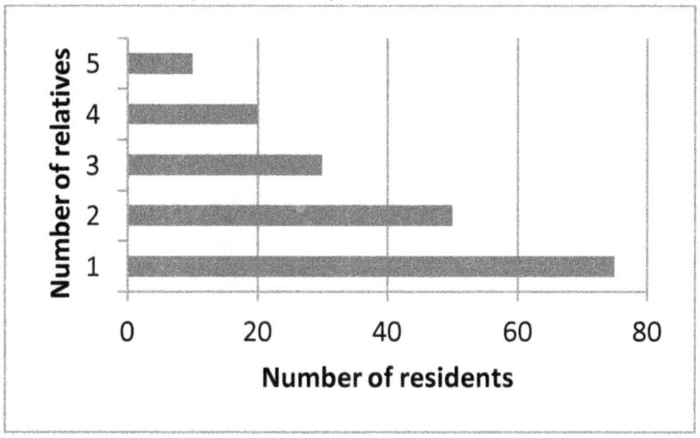

How many residents of Hendersonville had more than 3 relatives living within a ten-mile radius of the town?

A) 10
B) 20
C) 30
D) 155

8) The price of a wool coat is reduced 12.5% at the end of the winter. If the original price of the coat was $120, what will the price be after the reduction?

A) $108.00
B) $107.50
C) $105.70
D) $105.00

9) A motorcycle traveled 38.4 miles in $^4/_5$ of an hour. What was the speed of the motorcycle in miles per hour?

A) 9.6
B) 30.72
C) 48
D) 52

10) A factory that makes microchips produces 20 times as many functioning chips as defective chips. If the factory produced 11,235 chips in total last week, how many of them were defective?

A) 535
B) 561
C) 1,070
D) 10,700

11) A town has recently suffered a flood. The total cost, represented by variable C, which is available to accommodate *R* number of residents in emergency housing is represented by the equation C = $750R + $2,550. If the town has a total of $55,000 available for emergency housing, what is the greatest number of residents that it can house?

A) 68
B) 69
C) 70
D) 71

12) The following numbers are ordered from least to greatest: α, $^{2}/_{7}$, $^{8}/_{9}$, 1.35, $^{11}/_{3}$, μ
Which of the following could be the value of μ?

A) 3.5
B) $^{10}/_{4}$
C) 4.1
D) $^{1}/_{6}$

13) Find the median of the following numbers: 2.5, 9.4, 3.1, 1.7, 3.2, 8.2, 4.5, 6.4, 7.8

A) 3.2
B) 4.5
C) 5.2
D) 6.4

14) A student had these scores on exams during the semester: 89, 65, 75, 68, 82, 74, 86
What is the mean of his scores?

A) 24
B) 74
C) 75
D) 77

15) There are 10 cars in a parking lot. Nine of the cars are 2, 3, 4, 5, 6, 7, 9, 10, and 12 years old, respectively. If the average age of the 10 cars is 6 years old, how old is the 10th car?

A) 1 year old
B) 2 years old
C) 3 years old
D) 4 years old

16) The pictograph below shows the number of traffic violations that occur every week in a certain city. The fine for speeding violations is \$50 per violation. The fine for other violations is \$20 per violation. The total collected for all three types of violations was \$6,000. What is the fine for each parking violation?

Speeding	
Parking	
Other violations	

Each  represents 30 violations.

A) \$20
B) \$30
C) \$40
D) \$100

Algebra problems:

17) $(x^2 - x - 6) \div (x - 3) = ?$
A) x + 2
B) x – 2
C) y – 2
D) y + 2

18) Perform the operation: $(5ab - 6a)(3ab^3 - 4b^2 - 3a)$
A) $-15a^2b^4 - 20ab^3 - 15a^2b - 18a^2b^3 + 24ab^2 + 18a^2$
B) $15a^2b^4 - 20ab^3 - 15a^2b - 18a^2b^3 + 24ab^2 + 18a^2$
C) $15a^2b^4 - 20ab^3 - 15a^2b - 18a^2b^3 - 24ab^2 + 18a^2$
D) $15ab^4 - 20ab^3 - 15a^2b - 18a^2b^3 + 24ab^2 + 18a^2$

19) If $4(2x + 2) = 6(x - 1) + 21$, what is the value of x?
A) $^7/_2$
B) $^2/_7$
C) $^{23}/_2$
D) $^2/_{23}$

20) The price of a sofa at a local furniture store was x dollars on Wednesday this week. On Thursday, the price of the sofa was reduced by 10% of Wednesday's price. On Friday, the price of the sofa was reduced again by 15% of Thursday's price. Which of the following expressions can be used to calculate the price of the sofa on Friday?
A) $(0.25)\,x$
B) $(0.75)\,x$
C) $(0.10)(0.15)x$
D) $(0.90)(0.85)x$

21) If $2x + y = 6$ and $m - n = 2$, what is the value of $(4x + 2y)(4m - 4n)$?

A) 8

B) 12

C) 16

D) 96

22) $\dfrac{x + \frac{1}{5}}{\frac{1}{x}} = ?$

A) $x^2 + 5$

B) $\dfrac{x^3}{5}$

C) $x^2 + \dfrac{x}{5}$

D) $\dfrac{x}{x + \frac{1}{5}}$

23) If $\frac{1}{5}x + 3 = 5$, then $x = ?$

A) $\frac{8}{5}$

B) $-\frac{8}{5}$

C) 8

D) 10

24) Factor the following. Then simplify. $\dfrac{x^2 + 5x + 6}{x^2 + 6x + 8} \times \dfrac{x^2 + 4x}{x^2 + 8x + 15}$

A)

$\dfrac{5}{x + 5}$

B)

$\dfrac{x}{x + 5}$

C)

$$\frac{x+3}{x+4}$$

D)

$$\frac{x+4}{x+3}$$

25) A clothing store sells jackets and jeans at a discount during a sales period. T represents the number of jackets sold and N represents the number of jeans sold. The total amount of money the store collected for sales of jeans and jackets during the sales period was $4,000. The amount of money earned from selling jackets was one-third of that earned from selling jeans. The jeans sold for $20 a pair. How many pairs of jeans did the store sell during the sales period?

A) 15
B) 20
C) 150
D) 200

26) Which of the following is equivalent to the expression 36 – $2x$ for all values of x?

A) 6 + 2(15 – x)
B) 6(6 – $2x$)
C) 39 – (3 – $2x$)
D) 8(5 – $2x$) – 4

27) Carlos is going to buy a house. The total purchase price of the house is represented by variable H. He will pay D dollars immediately, and then he will make equal payments (P) each month for M months. If H = $300,000, P = $700 and M = 360, how much will Carlos pay immediately?

A) $38,000
B) $48,000
C) $58,000
D) $252,000

28) Which of the following equations is equivalent to $\frac{x}{5} \div \frac{9}{y}$?

A) $\frac{xy}{45}$

B) $\frac{9x}{5y}$

C) $\frac{1}{9} \times \frac{x}{5y}$

D) $\frac{1}{5} \times \frac{9}{5y}$

29) $\sqrt[3]{\frac{8}{27}} = ?$

A) $\frac{2}{3}$

B) $\frac{4}{9}$

C) $\frac{2}{9}$

D) $\frac{\sqrt{8}}{9}$

30) $\frac{\sqrt{48}}{3} + \frac{5\sqrt{5}}{6} = ?$

A) $\frac{4\sqrt{3} + 5\sqrt{5}}{6}$

B) $\frac{8\sqrt{3} + 5\sqrt{5}}{6}$

C) $\frac{\sqrt{48} + 5\sqrt{5}}{9}$

D) $\frac{6\sqrt{48} + 5\sqrt{5}}{18}$

31) For all $x \neq 0$ and $y \neq 0$, $\frac{4x}{1/xy} = ?$

A) $\frac{4x}{xy}$

B) $\frac{xy}{4x}$

C) $4x^2y$

D) $4xy$

32) $10a^2b^3c \div 2ab^2c^2 = ?$

A) $5c \div ab$

B) $5a \div bc$

C) $5ab \div c$
D) $5ac \div b$

33) If x and y are positive integers, the expression $\frac{1}{\sqrt{x}-\sqrt{y}}$ is equivalent to which of the following?

A) $\sqrt{x}-y$

B) $\sqrt{x}+y$

C) $\frac{\sqrt{x}-y}{1}$

D) $\frac{\sqrt{x}+\sqrt{y}}{x-y}$

34) $(2+\sqrt{6})^2$ = ?

A) 8

B) $8+2\sqrt{6}$

C) $10+2\sqrt{6}$

D) $10+4\sqrt{6}$

35) $\sqrt[3]{5} \times \sqrt[3]{7}$ = ?

A) $\sqrt[3]{13}$

B) $\sqrt[6]{13}$

C) $\sqrt[9]{13}$

D) $\sqrt[3]{35}$

36) What is the value of $\frac{x-3}{2-x}$ when x = 1?

A) 2
B) –2
C) $-^1/_2$
D) $-^1/_2$

37) $\sqrt{5}$ is equivalent to what number in exponential notation?

A) $5^{\frac{1}{4}}$

B) $5^{\frac{1}{2}}$

C) $\frac{5}{2^2}$

D) $\frac{\sqrt{1}}{5^2}$

Geometry and graphing problems:

38) The graph of a linear equation is shown below. Which one of the tables of values best represents the points on the graph?

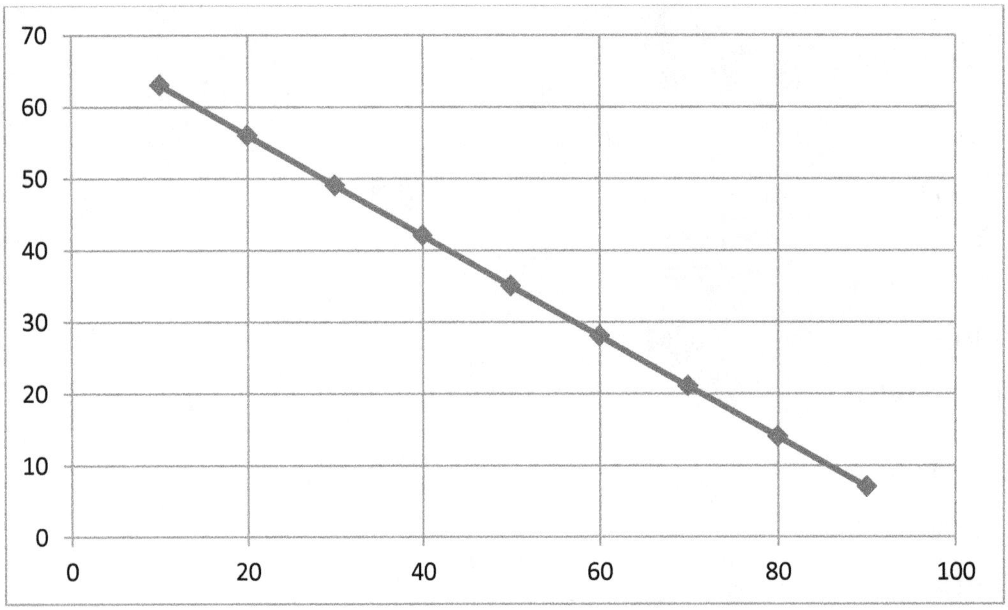

A)

x	y
5	65
10	64
15	63
20	62

B)

x	y
5	68
15	60
25	52
35	54

C)

x	y
10	63
20	56
30	49
40	42

D)

x	y
10	68
20	60
30	52
40	44

39) For the functions $f_2(x)$ listed below, x and y are integers greater than 1. If $f_1(x) = x^2$, which of the functions below has the greatest value for $f_1(f_2(x))$?

A) $f_2(x) = x/y$

B) $f_2(x) = xy$

C) $f_2(x) = y/x$

D) $f_2(x) = x - y$

40) The radius (R) of circle A is 5 centimeters. The radius of circle B is 3 centimeters. Which of the following statements is true?

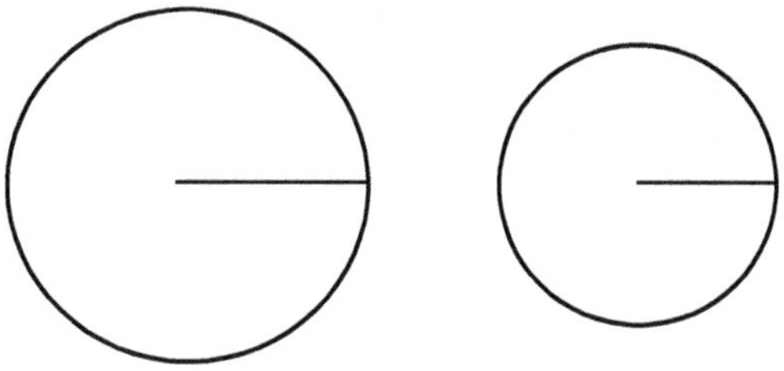

Circle A Circle B

A) The difference between the areas of the circles is 2.

B) The difference between the areas of the circles is 9π.

C) The difference between the circumferences of the circles is 2.

D) The difference between the circumferences of the circles is 4π.

41) Liz wants to put new vinyl flooring in her kitchen. She will buy the flooring in square pieces that measure 1 square foot each. The entire room is 8 feet by 12 feet. The cupboards are two feet deep from front to back. Flooring will not be put under the cupboards. A diagram of her kitchen is provided.

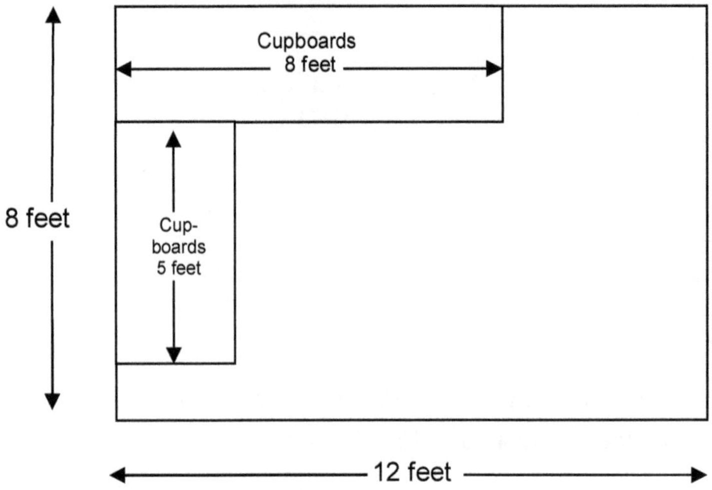

How many pieces of vinyl will Liz need to cover her floor?

A) 120
B) 96
C) 70
D) 84

42) A large wheel (L) has a radius of 10 inches. A small wheel (S) has a radius of 6 inches. If the large wheel is going to travel 360 revolutions, how many more revolutions does the small wheel need to make to cover the same distance?

A) 120
B) 240
C) 360
D) 720

43) Consider the vertex of an angle at the center of a circle. The diameter of the circle is 2. If the angle measures 90 degrees, what is the arc length relating to the angle?

A) $^{\pi}/_{2}$
B) $^{\pi}/_{4}$
C) 2π
D) 4π

44) A farmer has a rectangular pen in which he keeps animals. He has decided to divide the pen into two parts. To divide the pen, he will erect a fence diagonally from the two corners, as shown in the diagram below. How long in yards is the diagonal fence?

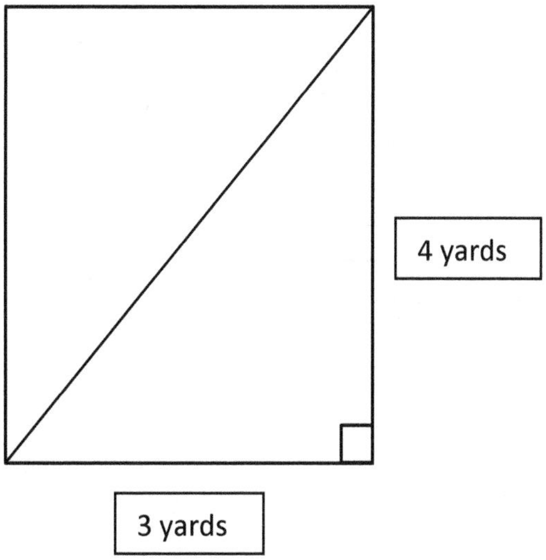

A) 4
B) 5
C) 5.5
D) 6

45) The diagram below shows a figure made from a semicircle, a rectangle, and an equilateral triangle. The rectangle has a length of 18 inches and a width of 10 inches. What is the perimeter of the figure?

A) 56 inches + 5π inches
B) 56 inches + 10π inches
C) 56 inches + 12.5π inches
D) 56 inches + 25π inches

46) The illustration below shows a pyramid with a base width of 3, a base length of 5, and a volume of 30. What is the height of the pyramid?

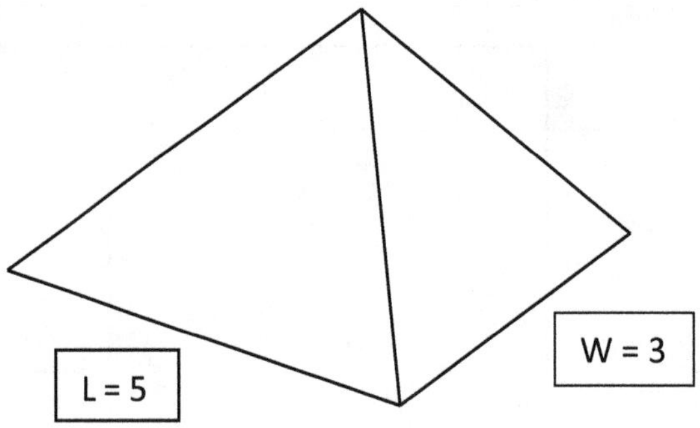

A) 2
B) 3
C) 5
D) 6

47) What is the area of the figure below?

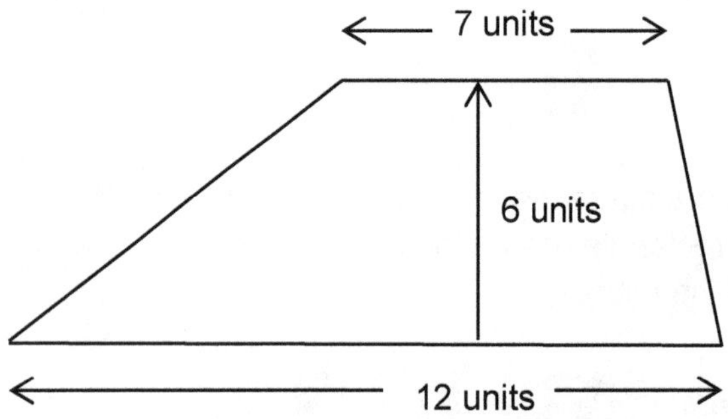

A) 57
B) 72
C) 84
D) 202

48) The illustration below shows a pentagon. The shaded part at the top of the pentagon has a height of 6 inches.

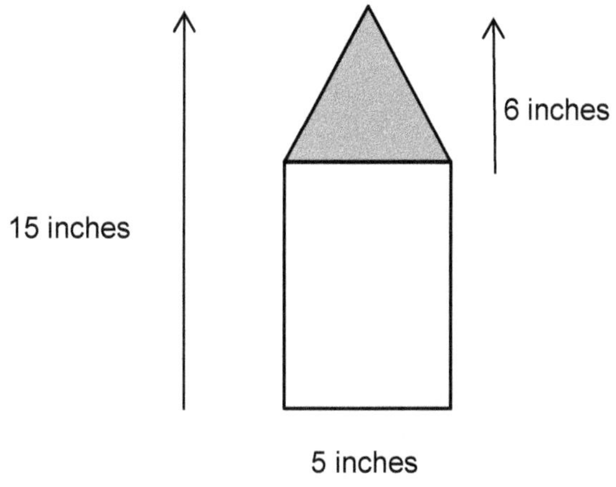

The height of the entire pentagon is 15 inches, and the base of the pentagon is 5 inches. What fraction expresses the area of the shaded part to the area of the entire pentagon?

A) $^{10}/_{45}$

B) $^{45}/_{10}$

C) $^{1}/_{4}$

D) $^{11}/_{2}$

49) A right triangle has two sides which have respective lengths of 5 and 3. The other side of the triangle is side x. Which of the following values could be the length of side x?

A) 2

B) $\sqrt{34}$

C) 8

D) $\sqrt{28}$

50) In the figure below, *x* and *y* are parallel lines, and line *z* is a transversal crossing both *x* and *y*. Which three angles are equal in measure?

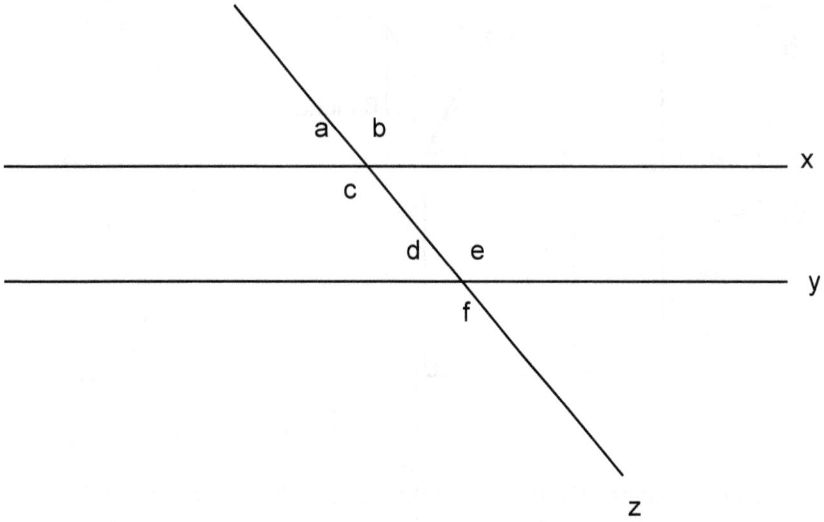

A) ∠a, ∠b, ∠c
B) ∠b, ∠c, ∠d
C) ∠b, ∠e, ∠f
D) ∠a, ∠d, ∠e

TABE Practice Math Test 4 – Answer Key

1) D
2) C
3) A
4) C
5) B
6) B
7) C
8) D
9) C
10) A
11) B
12) C
13) B
14) D
15) B
16) C
17) A
18) B
19) A
20) D
21) D
22) C
23) D
24) B
25) C
26) A
27) B
28) A
29) A
30) B
31) C
32) C
33) D
34) D

35) D

36) B

37) B

38) C

39) B

40) D

41) C

42) B

43) A

44) B

45) A

46) D

47) A

48) C

49) B

50) C

TABE Practice Math Test 4 – Solutions and Explanations

1) The correct answer is D. We have the following numbers in our problem:

0.0012
0.0253
0.2135
0.3152

If you still do not feel confident with decimals, remember that you can remove the decimal point and the zeroes after the decimal but before the other integers in order to see the answer more clearly.

12
253
2135
3152

2) The correct answer is C. If $\frac{x}{24}$ is between 8 and 9, x will need to be between 192 and 216, since $\frac{192}{24}$ =192 ÷ 24 = 8 and $\frac{216}{24}$ = 216 ÷ 24 = 9. 200 is the only number from the answer choices that is greater than 192 and less than 216.

3) The correct answer is A. The ratio of bags of apples to bags of oranges is 2 to 3, so for every two bags of apples, there are three bags of oranges. First, take the total amount of bags of apples and divide by 2: 44 ÷ 2 = 22. Then multiply this by 3 to determine how many bags of oranges are in the store: 22 × 3 = 66.

4) The correct answer is C. Work backwards based on the facts given. There are 18 students left at the end after one-fourth of them left for the principal's office. So, set up an equation for this:

$18 + {}^{1}/_{4}T = T$
$18 + {}^{1}/_{4}T - {}^{1}/_{4}T = T - {}^{1}/_{4}T$
$18 = {}^{3}/_{4}T$
$18 \times 4 = {}^{3}/_{4}T \times 4$
$72 = 3T$
$72 \div 3 = 3T \div 3$
$24 = T$

So, before the group of pupils left to see the principal, there were 24 students in the class. We know that one-fifth of the students left at the beginning to go to singing lessons, so we need to set up an equation for this:

$24 + {}^{1}/_{5}T = T$
$24 + {}^{1}/_{5}T - {}^{1}/_{5}T = T - {}^{1}/_{5}T$
$24 = {}^{4}/_{5}T$
$24 \times 5 = {}^{4}/_{5}T \times 5$
$120 = 4T$
$120 \div 4 = 4T \div 4$
$30 = T$

5) The correct answer is B. At the beginning of January, there are 300 students, but 5% of the students leave during the month, so we have 95% left at the end of the month: 300 × 95% = 285. Then 15 students join on the last day of the month, so we add that back in to get to the total at the end of January: 285 + 15 = 300. If this pattern continues, there will always be 300 students in the academy at the end of any month.

6) The correct answer is B. The question is asking us to calculate one third of one half. So, we multiply to get our answer: $^1/_2 \times {}^1/_3 = {}^{(1 \times 1)}/_{(2 \times 3)} = {}^1/_6$

7) The correct answer is C. The question is asking us how many residents have more than 3 relatives nearby, so we need to add the bars for 4 and 5 relatives from the chart. 20 residents have 4 relatives nearby and 10 residents have 5 relatives nearby, so 30 residents (20 + 10 = 30) have more than 3 relatives nearby.

8) The correct answer is D. Calculate the discount: $120 × 12.5% = $15 discount. Then subtract the discount from the original price to determine the sales price: $120 – $15 = $105

9) The correct answer is C. Divide by the fractional hour in order to determine the speed for an entire hour: 38.4 miles ÷ $^4/_5$ of an hour = 38.4 × $^5/_4$ = (38 × 5) ÷ 4 = 47.5 mph. This is rounded up to 48.

10) The correct answer is A. The ratio of defective chips to functioning chips is 1 to 20. So, the defective chips form one group and the functioning chips form another group. Therefore, the total data set can be divided into groups of 21. Accordingly, $^1/_{21}$ of the chips will be defective. The factory produced 11,235 chips last week, so we calculate as follows: 11,235 × $^1/_{21}$ = 535

11) The correct answer is B. The total amount available is $55,000, so we can substitute this for C in the equation provided in order to calculate *R* number of residents:
C = $750*R* + $2,550
$55,000 = $750*R* + $2,550
$55,000 – $2,550 = $750*R* + $2,550 – $2,550
$55,000 – $2,550 = $750*R*
$52,450 = $750*R*
$52,450 ÷ $750 = $750*R* ÷ $750
$52,450 ÷ $750 = *R*
69.9 = *R*

It is not possible to accommodate a fractional part of one person, so we need to round down to 69 residents.

12) The correct answer is C. The value of μ must be greater than $^{11}/_3$, which is equal to 3.6667. The answer 4.1 is the only option which meets this criterion.

13) The correct answer is B. Our data set is: 2.5, 9.4, 3.1, 1.7, 3.2, 8.2, 4.5, 6.4, 7.8. First, put the numbers in ascending order: 1.7, 2.5, 3.1, 3.2, 4.5, 6.4, 7.8, 8.2, 9.4. The median is the number in the middle of the set: 1.7, 2.5, 3.1, 3.2, **4.5**, 6.4, 7.8, 8.2, 9.4

14) The correct answer is D. To find the mean, add up all of the items in the set and then divide by the number of items in the set. Here we have 7 numbers in the set, so we get our answer as follows: (89 + 65 + 75 + 68 + 82 + 74 + 86) ÷ 7 = 539 ÷ 7 = 77

15) The correct answer is B. We don't know the age of the 10th car, so put this in as x to solve:
$(2 + 3 + 4 + 5 + 6 + 7 + 9 + 10 + 12 + x) \div 10 = 6$
$[(2 + 3 + 4 + 5 + 6 + 7 + 9 + 10 + 12 + x) \div 10] \times 10 = 6 \times 10$
$2 + 3 + 4 + 5 + 6 + 7 + 9 + 10 + 12 + x = 60$
$58 + x = 60$
$x = 2$

16) The correct answer is C. There are 2 stars for speeding, and each star equals 30 violations, so there were 60 speeding violations in total. The fine for speeding is \$50 per violation, so the total amount collected for speeding violations was: 60 speeding violations × \$50 per violation = \$3000. There are three stars for other violations, which is equal to 90 violations (3 × 30 = 90). Other violations are \$20 each, so the total for other violations is: 90 × \$20 = \$1800. Next, we need to deduct these two amounts from the total collections of \$6,000 in order to find out how much was collected for parking violations: \$6000 – \$3000 – \$1800 = \$1200 in total for parking violations. There is one star for parking violations, so there were 30 parking violations. We divide to get the answer: \$1200 income for parking violations ÷ 30 parking violations = \$40 each

17) The correct answer is A. In order to solve this type of problem, you must do long division of the quadratic. Remember that you are subtracting the terms when you perform each part of the long division, so you need to be careful with negatives.

$$\begin{array}{r} x + 2 \\ x - 3\overline{)x^2 - x - 6} \\ \underline{x^2 - 3x} \quad\;\; \\ 2x - 6 \\ \underline{2x - 6} \\ 0 \end{array}$$

18) The correct answer is B. Step 1: Apply the distributive property of multiplication by multiplying the first term in the first set of parentheses by all of the terms inside the second pair of parentheses. Then multiply the second term from the first set of parentheses by all of the terms inside the second set of parentheses.
$(5ab - 6a)(3ab^3 - 4b^2 - 3a) =$
$(5ab \times 3ab^3) + (5ab \times -4b^2) + (5ab \times -3a) + (-6a \times 3ab^3) + (-6a \times -4b^2) + (-6a \times -3a)$

Step 2: Add up the individual products in order to solve the problem:
$(5ab \times 3ab^3) + (5ab \times -4b^2) + (5ab \times -3a) + (-6a \times 3ab^3) + (-6a \times -4b^2) + (-6a \times -3a) =$
$15a^2b^4 - 20ab^3 - 15a^2b - 18a^2b^3 + 24ab^2 + 18a^2$

19) The correct answer is A. Perform the multiplication on the terms in the parentheses first.
$4(2x + 2) = 6(x - 1) + 21$
$8x + 8 = (6x - 6) + 21$

Then move the terms with x so that they are on just one side of the equation.
$8x + 8 = 6x + 15$

$8x - 6x + 8 = 6x - 6x + 15$
$2x + 8 = 15$

Then deal with the integers.
$2x + 8 - 8 = 15 - 8$
$2x = 7$

Then express as a fraction to solve the problem.
$x = {}^{7}/_{2}$

20) The correct answer is D. The original price of the sofa on Wednesday was x. On Thursday, the sofa was reduced by 10%, so the price on Thursday was 90% of x or $0.90x$. On Friday, the sofa was reduced by a further 15%, so the price on Friday was 85% of the price on Thursday, so we can multiply Thursday's price by 0.85 to get our answer: $(0.90)(0.85)x$

21) The correct answer is D. The problem tells us that $2x + y = 6$ and $m - n = 2$, so we need to factor the problem into those terms first of all.
$(4x + 2y)(4m - 4n) =$
$2(2x + y) \times 4(m - n)$

Then substitute the values provided into the equation.
$2(2x + y) \times 4(m - n) =$
$2(6) \times 4(2) =$
$(2 \times 6) \times (4 \times 2) =$
$12 \times 8 = 96$

22) The correct answer is C. Remember that a fraction can also be expressed as division.

In order to divide fractions, invert the second fraction and then multiply. To invert, swap the positions of the numerator and denominator in the second fraction. In this case $\frac{1}{x}$ becomes $\frac{x}{1}$ when inverted, which is then simplified to x.

$$\left(x + \frac{1}{5}\right) \div \frac{1}{x} =$$

$$\left(x + \frac{1}{5}\right) \times x =$$

$$x^2 + \frac{x}{5}$$

23) The correct answer is D. Get the integers to one side of the equation first of all.

$$\frac{1}{5}x + 3 = 5$$

$$\frac{1}{5}x + 3 - 3 = 5 - 3$$

$\frac{1}{5}x = 2$

Then multiply to eliminate the fraction and solve the problem.

$\frac{1}{5}x \times 5 = 2 \times 5$

$x = 10$

24) The correct answer is B. Here, we have quite an advanced problem. Be sure to study the steps below carefully if you had trouble finding the solution for this problem.

For this type of problem, first you need to find the factors of the numerators and denominators of each fraction. When there are only addition signs in the rational expression, the factors will be in the following format: (+)(+) If there is a negative sign, then the factors will be in this format: (+)(–) You have to find the factors of the terms containing *x* or *y* variables, as well as the factors of the integers or other constants. It is usually best to start with finding the factors of the final integer in each polynomial expression.

Step 1: The numerator of the first fraction is $x^2 + 5x + 6$, so the final integer is 6.
The factors of 6 are:
1 × 6 = 6
2 × 3 = 6
Add these factors together to discover what integer you need to use in front of the second term of the expression.
1 + 6 = 7
2 + 3 = 5
2 and 3 satisfy both parts of the equation. Therefore, the factors of $x^2 + 5x + 6$ are $(x+2)(x+3)$.

Step 2: Now factor the other parts of the problem. The denominator of the first fraction is $x^2 + 6x + 8$, so the final integer is 8.
The factors of 8 are:
1 × 8 = 8
2 × 4 = 8
Then add these factors together to find the integer to use in front of the second term of the expression.
1 + 8 = 9
2 + 4 = 6
Therefore, the factors of $x^2 + 6x + 8$ are $(x+2)(x+4)$.

Step 3: The numerator of the second fraction is $x^2 + 4x$, so there is no final integer. Because *x* is common to both terms of the expression, the factor will be in this format: *x*(*x* +). Therefore, in order to factor $x^2 + 4x$, we express it as $x(x+4)$.

Step 4: The denominator of the second fraction is $x^2 + 8x + 15$, so the final integer is 15.

The factors of 15 are:
1 × 15 = 15
3 × 5 = 15
Add these factors together to find the integer to use in front of the second term of the expression.
1 + 15 = 16
3 + 5 = 8
Therefore, the factors of $x^2 + 8x + 15$ are $(x+3)(x+5)$.

A good shortcut for this type of problem is to remind yourself that it is a problem about factoring, so the factors you find in step 1 will probably be common to other parts of the expression.
In other words, we discovered in step 1 that the factors of $x^2 + 5x + 6$ are $(x+2)$ and $(x+3)$.
So, when you are factoring out the other parts of the problem, start with $(x+2)$ and $(x+3)$.

Now that we have completed all of the four steps above, we can set out our problem with the factors we discovered in each step. We can see the factors of each fraction more clearly as show below.

$$\frac{x^2+5x+16}{x^2+6x+8} = \frac{(x+2)(x+3)}{(x+2)(x+4)} \qquad \frac{x^2+4x}{x^2+8x+15} = \frac{x(x+4)}{(x+3)(x+5)}$$

The problem should be set up as follows after you have found the factors:

$$\frac{x^2+5x+6}{x^2+6x+8} \times \frac{x^2+4x}{x^2+8x+15} =$$

$$\frac{(x+2)(x+3)}{(x+2)(x+4)} \times \frac{x(x+4)}{(x+3)(x+5)}$$

Then you need to simplify by removing the common factors. Remove $(x + 2)$ from the first fraction.

$$\frac{(x+2)(x+3)}{(x+2)(x+4)} \times \frac{x(x+4)}{(x+3)(x+5)} =$$

$$\frac{(x+3)}{(x+4)} \times \frac{x(x+4)}{(x+3)(x+5)}$$

Once you have simplified each fraction as much as possible, perform the operation indicated. In this problem, we are multiplying. So, we can express the two factored-out fractions as one fraction and then remove the other common terms.

$$\frac{(x+3)}{(x+4)} \times \frac{x(x+4)}{(x+3)(x+5)} =$$

$$\frac{(x+3)(x+4)x}{(x+4)(x+3)(x+5)}$$

You can remove $(x+3)$ from the above fraction since it is in both the numerator and denominator.

$$\frac{(x+3)(x+4)x}{(x+4)(x+3)(x+5)} =$$

$$\frac{(x+4)x}{(x+4)(x+5)}$$

We can further simplify by removing $(x+4)$.

$$\frac{(x+4)x}{(x+4)(x+5)} = \frac{x}{(x+5)}$$

So, our final answer is $\frac{x}{x+5}$

25) The correct answer is C. If the amount earned from selling jackets was one-third that of selling jeans, the ratio of jacket to jean sales was 1 to 3. So, we need to divide the total sales of \$4,000 into \$1,000 for jackets and \$3,000 for jeans. We can then solve the problem as follows: \$3,000 in jeans sales ÷ \$20 per pair = 150 pairs sold

26) The correct answer is A. For algebraic equivalency questions like this, you can perform the operations on each of the answer choices to see which one is equivalent. Remember to be careful when performing multiplication on negative numbers inside parentheticals.

$6 + 2(15 - x) =$

$6 + (2 \times 15) + (2 \times -x) =$

$6 + 30 - 2x =$

$36 - 2x$

27) The correct answer is B. The total of the monthly payments is: \$700 per month × 360 months = \$252,000. The total price of the house is \$300,000 so deduct the total payments from this amount in order to calculate the immediate payment: \$300,000 – \$252,000 = \$48,000

28) The correct answer is A. To divide, invert the second fraction and then multiply as shown.

$$\frac{x}{5} \div \frac{9}{y} = \frac{x}{5} \times \frac{y}{9} = \frac{x \times y}{5 \times 9} = \frac{xy}{45}$$

29) The correct answer is A. Find the cube roots of the integers and then factor the integers. The cube root is the number which satisfies the equation when it is multiplied by itself two times.

$$\sqrt[3]{\frac{8}{27}} = \sqrt[3]{\frac{2 \times 2 \times 2}{3 \times 3 \times 3}}$$

Then express the result as a rational number.

$$\sqrt[3]{\frac{2\times2\times2}{3\times3\times3}}=\frac{2}{3}$$

30) The correct answer is B. Find the lowest common denominator.

$$\frac{\sqrt{48}}{3}+\frac{5\sqrt{5}}{6}=$$

$$\left(\frac{\sqrt{48}}{3}\times\frac{2}{2}\right)+\frac{5\sqrt{5}}{6}=$$

$$\frac{2\sqrt{48}}{6}+\frac{5\sqrt{5}}{6}$$

Then simplify, if possible.

$$\frac{2\sqrt{48}}{6}+\frac{5\sqrt{5}}{6}=$$

$$\frac{2\sqrt{16\times3}+5\sqrt{5}}{6}=$$

$$\frac{2\sqrt{(4\times4)\times3}+5\sqrt{5}}{6}=$$

$$\frac{(2\times4)\sqrt{3}+5\sqrt{5}}{6}=$$

$$\frac{8\sqrt{3}+5\sqrt{5}}{6}$$

31) The correct answer is C. When the denominator of a fraction contains another fraction, treat the main fraction as the division sign.

$$\frac{4x}{1/xy}=4x\div 1/xy$$

Then invert and multiply as usual.

$$4x \div \frac{1}{xy} = 4x \times \frac{xy}{1}$$

$$4x \times \frac{xy}{1} = 4x \times xy$$

$$4x \times xy = 4x^2 y$$

32) The correct answer is C. First perform the division on the integers: $10 \div 2 = 5$

Then do the division on the other variables.
$a^2 \div a = a$
$b^3 \div b^2 = b$

$c \div c^2 = \frac{1}{c}$

Then multiply these together to get the solution.

$$5 \times a \times b \times \frac{1}{c} =$$

$$\frac{5ab}{c} = 5ab \div c$$

33) The correct answer is D. First of all, you have to eliminate the radicals in the denominator by factoring. When you have two different variables in a rational expression such as *x* and *y* and your second variable is negative, the factored equation will be in the format (+)(–). We know that one sign will be positive and the other will be negative when we factor because we can get a negative product only when we multiply a positive number with a negative number. So, we will multiply the denominator as follows:

$$\left(\sqrt{x}+\sqrt{y}\right)\left(\sqrt{x}-\sqrt{y}\right)$$

We can swap the order of the sets of parentheses to make the multiplication a bit easier to follow.

$$\left(\sqrt{x}+\sqrt{y}\right)\left(\sqrt{x}-\sqrt{y}\right)=$$
$$\left(\sqrt{x}-\sqrt{y}\right)\left(\sqrt{x}+\sqrt{y}\right)$$

Now we are ready to solve the problem.

$$\frac{1}{\sqrt{x}-\sqrt{y}} =$$

$$\frac{1}{\sqrt{x}-\sqrt{y}} \times \frac{\sqrt{x}+\sqrt{y}}{\sqrt{x}+\sqrt{y}}$$

Simplify the numerator and multiply the radicals in the denominator by using the FOIL method.

$$\frac{1}{\sqrt{x}-\sqrt{y}} \times \frac{\sqrt{x}+\sqrt{y}}{\sqrt{x}+\sqrt{y}} =$$

$$\frac{\sqrt{x}+\sqrt{y}}{\sqrt{x}^2+\sqrt{xy}-\sqrt{xy}-\sqrt{y}^2} =$$

$$\frac{\sqrt{x}+\sqrt{y}}{(\sqrt{x})^2-(\sqrt{y})^2}$$

Then simplify the denominator.

$$\frac{\sqrt{x}+\sqrt{y}}{(\sqrt{x})^2-(\sqrt{y})^2} =$$

$$\frac{\sqrt{x}+\sqrt{y}}{x-y}$$

34) The correct answer is D. Don't worry about the radical. This is just another type of FOIL problem.

$(2+\sqrt{6})^2 =$

$(2+\sqrt{6})(2+\sqrt{6}) =$

First . . . Outside . . Inside . . . Last

$(2\times 2)+(2\times\sqrt{6})+(2\times\sqrt{6})+(\sqrt{6}\times\sqrt{6}) =$

$(2\times 2)+(2\sqrt{6}+2\sqrt{6})+\sqrt{6}^2 =$

$4+4\sqrt{6}+6 =$

$10+4\sqrt{6}$

35) The correct answer is D. Remember for problems like this, you need to multiply the amounts inside the radical sign, but leave the cube root as it is. $\sqrt[3]{5}\times\sqrt[3]{7}=\sqrt[3]{35}$

36) The correct answer is B.

Substitute 1 for *x*.

$$\frac{x-3}{2-x} =$$

$$\frac{1-3}{2-1} =$$

$(1-3)\div(2-1) =$

$-2 \div 1 = -2$

37) The correct answer is B. Remember that $\sqrt{x} = x^{\frac{1}{2}}$. So, $\sqrt{5} = 5^{\frac{1}{2}}$

38) The correct answer is C. The first point on the graph lies at x = 10, so we can eliminate answer choices A and B. The point for the y coordinate that corresponds to x = 10 is 63 not 68, so we can eliminate answer choice D.

39) The correct answer is B. Two whole numbers that are greater than 1 will always result in a greater number when they are multiplied by each other, rather than when those numbers are divided by each other or subtracted from each other.

40) The correct answers is D. The formula for the area of a circle is: πR^2. The area of circle A is $\pi \times 5^2 = 25\pi$ and the area of circle B is $\pi \times 3^2 = 9\pi$. So, the difference between the areas is 16π. The formula for circumference is: $\pi 2R$. The circumference of circle A is $\pi \times 2 \times 5 = 10\pi$ and the circumference for circle B is $\pi \times 2 \times 3 = 6\pi$. The difference in the circumferences is 4π. So, answer D is correct.

41) The correct answer is C. Calculate the area for each cupboard: 8 × 2 = 16 and 5 × 2 = 10. Therefore, the total area for both cupboards is 16 + 10 = 26. Then find the area for the entire kitchen: 8 × 12 = 96. Then deduct the cupboards from the total: 96 – 26 = 70

42) The correct answer is B. Circumference is $2\pi R$, so the circumference of the large wheel is 20π and the circumference of the smaller wheel is 12π. If the large wheel travels 360 revolutions, it travels a distance of: $20\pi \times 360 = 7200\pi$. To determine the number of revolutions the small wheel needs to make to go the same distance, we divide the distance by the circumference of the smaller wheel: $7200\pi \div 12\pi = 600$. Finally, calculate the difference in the number of revolutions: $600 - 360 = 240$

43) The correct answer is A. For questions like this on arcs, you should first find the circumference of the circle. The diameter of the circle is 2, so the circumference is 2π. There are 360 degrees in a circle and the question is asking us about a 90 degree angle, so the arc length relates to one-fourth of the circumference: 90 ÷ 360 = $^1/_4$. So, we need to take one-fourth of the circumference to get the answer: $2\pi \times {}^1/_4 = {}^{2\pi}/_4 = {}^{\pi}/_2$

44) The correct answer is B. The two sides of the field form a right angle, so we can use the Pythagorean Theorem to solve the problem: $\sqrt{3^2 + 4^2} = \sqrt{9 + 16} = \sqrt{25} = 5$

45) The correct answer is A. First, we need to find the circumference of the semicircle on the left side of the figure. The width of the rectangle of 10 inches forms the diameter of the semicircle, so the circumference of an entire circle with a diameter of 10 inches would be 10π inches. We need the circumference for a semicircle only, which is half of a circle, so we need to divide the circumference by 2: $10\pi \div 2 = 5\pi$. Since the right side of the figure is an equilateral triangle, the two sides of the triangle have the same length as the width of the rectangle, so they are 10 inches each. Finally, you need to add up the lengths of all of the sides to get the answer: 18 + 18 + 10 + 10 + 5π = 56 + 5π inches

46) The correct answer is D. To solve the problem, insert the values provided in the problem into the formula for the volume of a pyramid: $\frac{1}{3}$ × length × width × height

$\frac{1}{3}$ × length × width × height = 30

$\frac{1}{3}$ × 5 × 3 × height = 30

$\frac{15}{3}$ × height = 30

5 × height = 30

5 ÷ 5 × height = 30 ÷ 5

height = 6

47) The correct answer is A. Since the left and right sides of this figure are not parallel, the figure is classified as a trapezoid. To find the area of a trapezoid we take the average of the length of the top (T) and bottom (B) and multiply by the height (H):

$\frac{T+B}{2} \times H =$

$\frac{7+12}{2} \times 6 =$

$9.5 \times 6 = 57$

48) The correct answer is C. Calculate the area of the triangle: $\frac{1}{2} \times base \times height = \frac{1}{2} \times 5 \times 6 = \frac{1}{2} \times 30 = 15$. The height of the unshaded part is 9 inches since $15 - 6 = 9$, so next we can calculate the area of the unshaded rectangular part: $base \times height = 5 \times 9 = 45$. Add the area of the unshaded part of the figure to the area of the triangle in order to get the area for the entire figure: $45 + 15 = 60$. Finally, express the result as a simplified fraction with the area of the triangle in the numerator and the area of the entire figure in the denominator: ${}^{15}/_{60} = {}^{1}/_{4}$

49) The correct answer is B. Here we have a right triangle with three sides, the measurements of which are 3, 5, and an unknown length that we will call x. We do not know which of the lengths represents the hypotenuse, so we have to use the Pythagorean Theorem for three scenarios:

<u>Hypotenuse = x</u>

$\sqrt{3^2 + 5^2} = x$

$\sqrt{9 + 25} = x$

$\sqrt{34} = x$

<u>Hypotenuse = 5</u>

$\sqrt{3^2 + x^2} = 5$

$\sqrt{9 + x^2} = 5$

Then square both sides of the equation to eliminate the radical.
$(\sqrt{9+x^2})^2 = 5^2$
$9+ x^2 = 25$
$x^2 = 25 - 9$
$x^2 = 16$
$x = 4$

<u>Hypotenuse = 3</u>
$\sqrt{5^2 + x^2} = 3$
$\sqrt{25 + x^2} = 3$
Then square both sides of the equation to eliminate the radical.
$(\sqrt{25+x^2})^2 = 9$
$25+ x^2 = 9$
$x^2 = 9 - 25$
$x^2 = -16$
Real number square roots do not exist for negative numbers, so the hypotenuse cannot have a length of 3 in this problem.

50) The correct answer is C. When a transversal crosses two parallel lines, opposite angles will be equal in measure and corresponding angles will also be equal in measure. (Corresponding angles are angles in the matching same-shaped corners.) Angles ∠b and ∠e are corresponding and angles ∠e and ∠f are opposite, so answer C is correct.

TABE Math Practice Test 5

Number and data problems:

1) $82 + 9 \div 3 - 5 = ?$
   A) –40.50
   B) 40.50
   C) 80.00
   D) 85.33

2) $52 + 6 \times 3 - 48 = ?$
   A) 22
   B) 82
   C) 126
   D) 322

3) Convert the following to decimal format: $^{3}/_{20}$
   A) 0.0015
   B) 0.015
   C) 0.15
   D) 0.66

4) 60 is 20 percent of what number?
   A) 80
   B) 120
   C) 1200
   D) 300

5) $6^{3}/_{4} - 2^{1}/_{2} = ?$
   A) $4^{1}/_{4}$
   B) $4^{3}/_{8}$
   C) $4^{5}/_{8}$
   D) $4^{6}/_{8}$

6) $9 \times 6 + 42 \div 6 = ?$
   A) 8
   B) 16
   C) 27
   D) 61

7) Find the value of *x* that solves the following proportion: $^{9}/_{6} = ^{x}/_{10}$
   A) 1.5
   B) 15
   C) .67
   D) 67

8) Susan wanted to find the mean of the six tests she has taken this semester. However, she erroneously divided the total points from the six tests by 5, which gave her a result of 96. What is the correct mean of her six tests?
A) 63
B) 80
C) 82
D) 91

9) $^{1}/_{8} \div {}^{4}/_{3} = ?$
A) $^{1}/_{6}$
B) $^{32}/_{3}$
C) $^{3}/_{24}$
D) $^{3}/_{32}$

10) A group of friends are trying to lose weight. Person A lost $14^{3}/_{4}$ pounds. Person B lost $20^{1}/_{5}$ pounds. Person C lost 36.35 pounds. What is the total weight loss for the group?
A) 71.30
B) 70.475
C) 71.05
D) 71.15

11) Convert the following fraction to decimal format: $^{5}/_{50}$
A) 0.0010
B) 0.0100
C) 0.1000
D) 0.0500

12) One hundred students took an English test. The 55 female students in the class had an average score of 87, while the 45 male students in the class had an average of 80. What is the average test score for all 100 students in the class?
A) 82.00
B) 83.15
C) 83.50
D) 83.85

13) $3^{1}/_{2} - 2^{3}/_{5} = ?$
A) $^{9}/_{10}$
B) $1^{1}/_{10}$
C) $1^{1}/_{3}$
D) $1^{2}/_{3}$

14) $^{1}/_{6} + (^{1}/_{2} \div {}^{3}/_{8}) - (^{1}/_{3} \times {}^{3}/_{2}) = ?$
A) $^{23}/_{6}$
B) 1
C) 2
D) $^{1}/_{10}$

15) Mary needs to get \$650 in donations. So far, she has obtained 80% of the money she needs. How much money does she still need?
A) \$8.19
B) \$13.00
C) \$32.50
D) \$130.00

16) The Abdul family is shopping at a superstore. They buy product A and product B. Product A costs \$5 each, and product B costs \$8 each. They buy 4 of product A. They also buy a certain quantity of product B. The total value of their purchase is \$60. How many units of product B did they buy?
A) 4
B) 5
C) 6
D) 8

17) The price of socks is \$2 per pair and the price of shoes is \$25 per pair. Anna went shopping for socks and shoes, and she paid \$85 in total. In this purchase, she bought 3 pairs of shoes. How many pairs of socks did she buy?
A) 2
B) 3
C) 5
D) 8

Algebra problems:

18) For all positive integers x and y, $x - 6 < 0$ and $y < x + 12$, then $y <$?
A) 6
B) 12
C) 18
D) 24

19) Which of the following is the number line of the solution of $2 + y < -8$?

A)

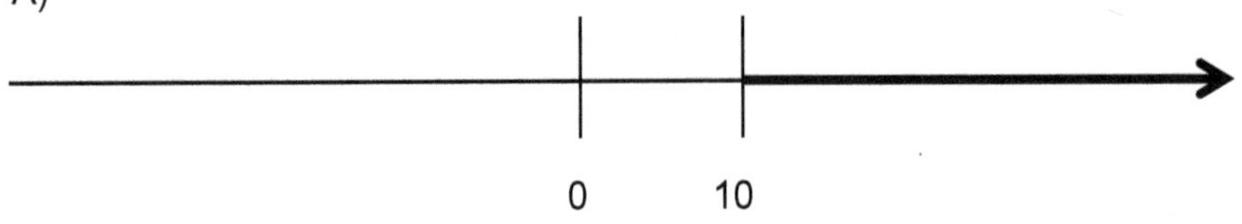

B)

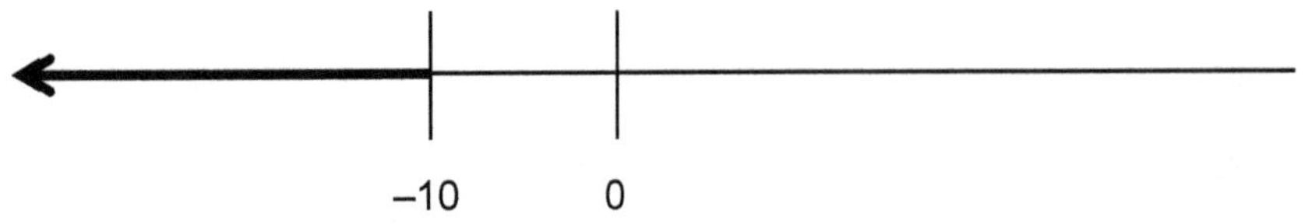

C)

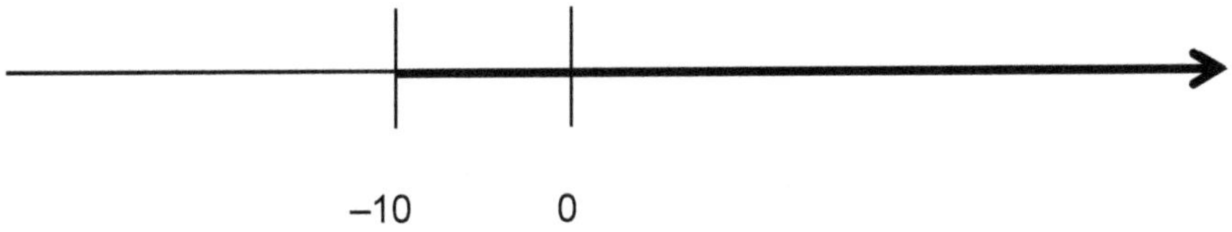

D)

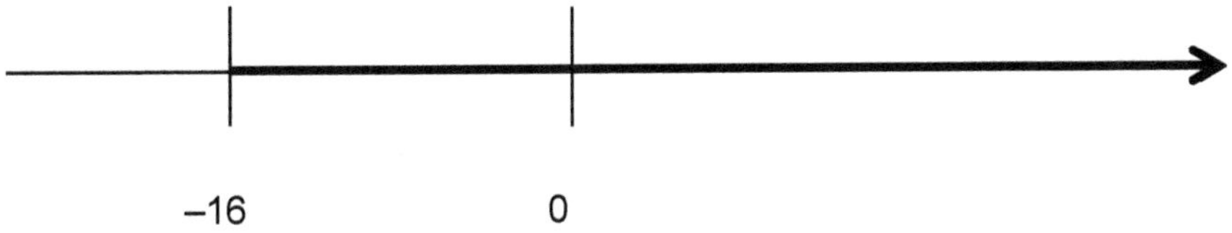

20) $(6y)^0 = ?$

A) $6y$
B) 6
C) 1
D) 0

21) $\sqrt{14x^5} \times \sqrt{6x^3} = ?$

A) $\sqrt{20x^{15}}$
B) $\sqrt{84x^{15}}$
C) $2x^4\sqrt{21}$
D) $2x^8\sqrt{21}$

22) $8ab^2(3ab^4 + 2b) = ?$

A) $24a^2b^6 + 16ab^3$
B) $24a^2b^8 + 16ab^3$
C) $48ab^6 + 32ab^2$
D) $24ab^6 + 16ab^3$

23) Perform the operation and express as one fraction: $\frac{5}{12x} + \frac{4}{10x^2} = ?$

A) $\frac{9}{22x^3}$

B) $\frac{48x}{50x^2}$

C) $\frac{29}{12x}$

D) $\frac{25x+24}{60x^2}$

24) $(-5)^{-2}$ = ?

A) –25

B) $-\frac{1}{25}$

C) $\frac{1}{25}$

D) 25

25) Solve by elimination.

$x+5y=24$

$8x+2y=40$

A) (4, 4)

B) (–4,4)

C) (40,4)

D) (4,38)

26) Perform the operation: $(4x-3)(5x^2+12x+11)=?$

A) $20x^3+33x^2+80x-33$

B) $20x^3+33x^2+80x+33$

C) $20x^3+33x^2+8x-33$

D) $20x^3+33x^2-8x-33$

27) $\sqrt{6x^3}\sqrt{24x^5}=?$

A) $12\sqrt{x^{15}}$

B) $\sqrt{30x^8}$

C) $12x^4$

D) $144x^4$

28) $\sqrt{18}+3\sqrt{32}+5\sqrt{8}=?$

A) $17\sqrt{2}$

B) $25\sqrt{2}$

C) $8\sqrt{58}$

D) $15\sqrt{58}$

29) For all $a \neq b$, $\dfrac{\frac{5a}{b}}{\frac{2a}{a-b}} = ?$

A) $\dfrac{10a^2}{ab-b^2}$

B) $\dfrac{a-b}{2b}$

C) $\dfrac{5a-5}{2}$

D) $\dfrac{5a-5b}{2b}$

30) Perform the operation and express as one fraction: $\dfrac{1}{a+1}+\dfrac{1}{a}$

A) $\dfrac{2}{2a+1}$

B) $\dfrac{a+1}{a}$

C) $\dfrac{a^2+a}{2a+1}$

D) $\dfrac{2a+1}{a^2+a}$

Geometry and graphing problems:

31) What equation represents the slope-intercept formula for the following data?

Through (4, 5); $m = -3/5$

A) $y=-\dfrac{3}{5}x+5$

B) $y=-\dfrac{12}{5}x-5$

C) $y=-\dfrac{3}{5}x+\dfrac{37}{5}$

D) $y=-\dfrac{37}{5}x+\dfrac{3}{5}$

32) Find the midpoint between the following coordinates: (2, 2) and (4, –6)
A) (3,4)
B) (3,–4)
C) (3,2)
D) (3,–2)

33) In the standard (x, y) plane, what is the distance between $(3\sqrt{3},-1)$ and $(6\sqrt{3},2)$?
A) 6
B) 27
C) 36
D) $3\sqrt{3}+1$

34) The perimeter of a rectangle is 48 meters. If the length were doubled and the width were increased by 5 meters, the perimeter would be 92 meters. What are the length and width of the original rectangle?
A) width = 7, length = 17
B) width = 17, length = 7
C) width = 34, length = 14
D) width = 24, length = 46

35) In the figure below, the circle centered at B is internally tangent to the circle centered at A. The length of line segment AB, which represents the radius of circle A, is 3 units and the smaller circle passes through the center of the larger circle. If the area of the smaller circle is removed from the larger circle, what is the remaining area of the larger circle?

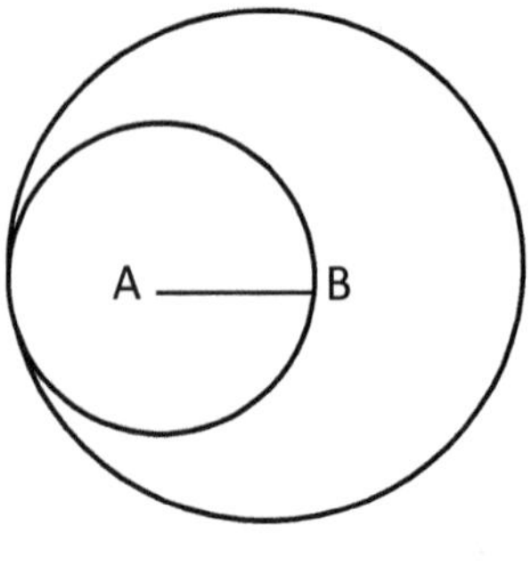

A) 3π
B) 6π
C) 9π
D) 27π

36) The perimeter of the square shown below is 24 units. What is the length of line segment AB?

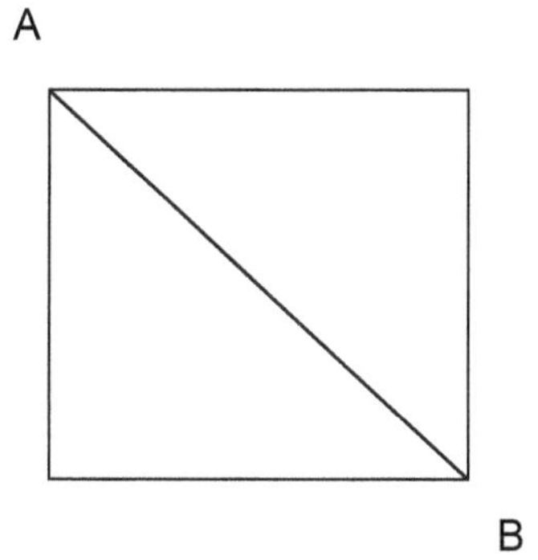

A) $\sqrt{24}$

B) $\sqrt{36}$

C) $\sqrt{72}$

D) 6

37) If a circle has a radius of 4, what is the circumference of the circle?

A) $\pi/8$

B) $\pi/16$

C) 8π

D) 16π

38) If a circle has a radius of 6, what is the area of the circle?

A) 6π

B) 12π

C) 24π

D) 36π

39) If circle A has a radius of 0.4 and circle B has a radius of 0.2, what is the difference in area between the two circles?

A) $.04\pi$

B) $.12\pi$

C) $.16\pi$

D) $.40\pi$

40) A rectangular box has a base that is 5 inches wide and 6 inches long. The height of the box is 10 inches. What is the volume of the box?

A) 30

B) 110

C) 150

D) 300

41) Consider a right-angled triangle, where side M and side N form the right angle, and side L is the hypotenuse. If M = 3 and N = 2, what is the length of side L?

A) 5

B) $\sqrt{5}$

C) $\sqrt{13}$

D) $\sqrt{15}$

42) Find the area of the right triangle whose base is 2 and height is 5.

A) 2.5

B) 5

C) 10

D) 15

43) Consider a right-angled triangle, where side A and side B form the right angle, and side C is the hypotenuse. If A = 5 and C = $\sqrt{34}$, what is the length of side B?

A) 8

B) 3

C) 34

D) $\sqrt{34}$

44) Consider the vertex of an angle at the center of a circle. The radius of the circle is 6. If the angle measures 30 degrees, what is the arc length relating to the angle?

A) π

B) 2π

C) 3π

D) 4π

45) Find the volume of a cone which has a radius of 3 and a height of 4.

A) 4π

B) 12π

C) $^{4\pi}/_{3}$

D) $^{3\pi}/_{4}$

46) Pat wants to put wooden trim around the floor of her family room. Each piece of wood is 1 foot in length. The room is rectangular and is 12 feet long and 10 feet wide. How many pieces of wood does Pat need for the entire perimeter of the room?

A) 22

B) 44

C) 100

D) 120

47) The Johnson's have decided to remodel their upstairs. They currently have 4 rooms upstairs that measure 10 feet by 10 feet each. When they remodel, they will make one large room that will be 20 feet by 10 feet and two small rooms that will each be 10 feet by 8 feet. The remaining space is to be allocated to a new bathroom. What are the dimensions of the new bathroom?

A) 4×10
B) 8×10
C) 10×10
D) 4×8

48) In the figure below, XY and WZ are parallel, and lengths are provided in units. What is the area of trapezoid WXYZ in square units?

A) 24
B) 30
C) 34
D) 36

49) In the figure below, the lengths of KL, LM, and KN are provided in units. What is the area of triangle NLM in square units?

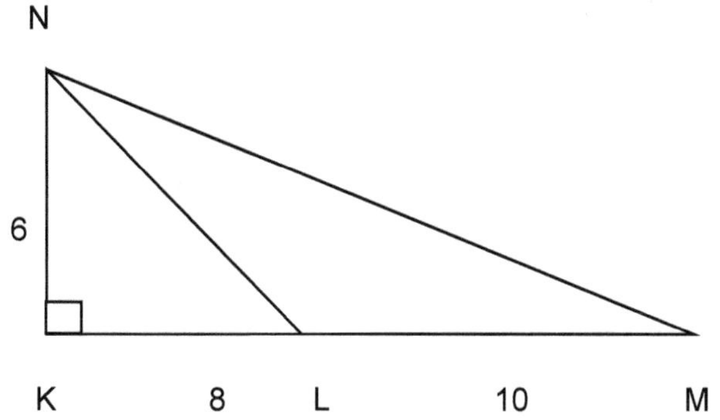

A) 24
B) 30
C) 48
D) 54

50) $\angle XYZ$ is an isosceles triangle, where XY is equal to YZ. Angle Y is 30° and points W, X, and Z are co-linear. What is the measurement of $\angle WXY$?

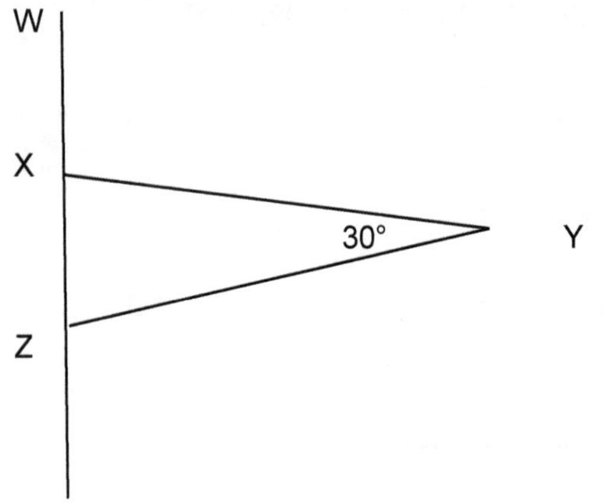

A) 40
B) 105
C) 150
D) 160

TABE Practice Math Test 5 – Answer Key

1) C
2) A
3) C
4) D
5) A
6) D
7) B
8) B
9) D
10) A
11) C
12) D
13) A
14) B
15) D
16) B
17) C
18) C
19) B
20) C
21) C
22) A
23) D
24) C
25) A
26) C
27) C
28) B
29) D
30) D
31) C
32) D
33) A
34) A
35) D

36) C
37) C
38) D
39) B
40) D
41) C
42) B
43) B
44) A
45) B
46) B
47) A
48) D
49) B
50) B

TABE Practice Math Test 5 – Solutions and Explanations

1) The correct answer is C. Remember that the order of operations is PEMDAS: Parentheses, Exponents, Multiplication, Division, Addition, and Subtraction.
In this problem, there are no operations with parentheses, exponents, or multiplication.
So, do the division first: $9 \div 3 = 3$
Then replace this in the equation: $82 + 9 \div 3 - 5 = 82 + 3 - 5 = 80$

2) The correct answer is A. This is another problem on the order of operations.
There are no operations with parentheses or exponents, so do the multiplication first.
$6 \times 3 = 18$

Then put this number in the equation.
$52 + 6 \times 3 - 48 =$
$52 + 18 - 48 = 22$

3) The correct answer is C. In order to convert a fraction to a decimal, you must divide.

```
   .15
20)3.00
    2.0
    1.00
    1.00
       0
```

4) The correct answer is D. 20 percent is equal to 0.20. The phrase "of what number" indicates that we need to divide the two amounts given in the problem: $60 \div 0.20 = 300$
We can check this result as follows: $300 \times 0.20 = 60$

5) The correct answer is A. Questions like this test your knowledge of mixed numbers. Mixed numbers are those that contain a whole number and a fraction. If the fraction on the first mixed number is greater than the fraction on the second mixed number, you can subtract the whole numbers and the fractions separately. Remember to use the lowest common denominator on the fractions. First, subtract whole numbers: $6 - 2 = 4$

Then subtract fractions.
$^3/_4 - {}^1/_2 =$
$^3/_4 - {}^2/_4 =$
$^1/_4$

Now put them together for the result.
$4\,^1/_4$

Alternatively, do the operations as follows:
$6\,^3/_4 - 2\,^1/_2 =$
$6\,^3/_4 - [2 + (^1/_2 \times {}^2/_2)] =$
$6\,^3/_4 - 2\,^2/_4 = 4\,^1/_4$

6) The correct answer is D. Remember PEMDAS: Parentheses, Exponents, Multiplication, Division, Addition, and Subtraction. So, you must do the division and multiplication first, before adding or subtracting: $9 \times 6 + 42 \div 6 = (9 \times 6) + (42 \div 6)$
We know that $9 \times 6 = 54$ and $42 \div 6 = 7$ so perform the operations and simplify:
$(9 \times 6) + (42 \div 6) = 54 + 7 = 61$

7) The correct answer is B. You can simplify the first fraction because both the numerator and denominator are divisible by 3: $^9/_6 \div {}^3/_3 = {}^3/_2$
Then divide the denominator of the second fraction by the denominator 2 of the simplified fraction $^3/_2$ from above: $10 \div 2 = 5$
Now, multiply this number by the numerator of the first fraction to get your result: $5 \times 3 = 15$
You can check your answer as follows:
$^9/_6 = {}^{15}/_{10}$
$^9/_6 \div {}^3/_3 = {}^3/_2$
$^{15}/_{10} \div {}^5/_5 = {}^3/_2$

8) The correct answer is B. First you need to find the total points that Susan earned. You do this by taking her erroneous average times 5: $5 \times 96 = 480$. Then you need to divide the total points earned by the correct number of tests to get the correct average: $480 \div 6 = 80$

9) The correct answer is D. When you are asked to divide fractions, remember that you need to invert the second fraction. Then you multiply this inverted fraction by the first fraction given in the problem. $^4/_3$ inverted is $^3/_4$. Then multiply the numerators and the denominators together to get the new fraction.

$$\frac{1}{8} \div \frac{4}{3} =$$

$$\frac{1}{8} \times \frac{3}{4} = \frac{3}{32}$$

10) The correct answer is A. Convert the fractions in the mixed numbers to decimals.
$^3/_4 = 3 \div 4 = 0.75$
$^1/_5 = 1 \div 5 = 0.20$

Then represent the mixed numbers as decimal numbers.
Person 1: $14^3/_4 = 14.75$
Person 2: $20^1/_5 = 20.20$
Person 3: 36.35

Then add all three amounts together to find the total.
$14.75 + 20.20 + 36.35 = 71.30$

11) The correct answer is C. Remember that to represent a fraction as a decimal, you need to divide. So, you will need to do long division to determine the answer.

$$\begin{array}{r} .10 \\ 50\overline{)5.00} \\ \underline{5.00} \\ 0 \end{array}$$

12) The correct answer is D. First of all, you have to calculate the total amount of points earned by the entire class. Multiply the female average by the amount of female students.
Total points for female students: $87 \times 55 = 4785$
Then multiply the male average by the amount of male students.
Total points for male students: $80 \times 45 = 3600$
Then add these two amounts together to find out the total points scored by the entire class.
Total points for entire class: $4785 + 3600 = 8385$
When you have calculated the total amount of points for the entire class, you divide this by the total number of students in the class to get the class average.
$8385 \div 100 = 83.85$

13) The correct answer is A. This question assesses your knowledge of mixed numbers.
In this problem, the fraction on the second number is bigger than the fraction on the first number. So, we have to convert the mixed numbers to fractions first.

$$3\frac{1}{2} - 2\frac{3}{5} =$$

$$\left[\left(3\times\frac{2}{2}\right)+\frac{1}{2}\right]-\left[\left(2\times\frac{5}{5}\right)+\frac{3}{5}\right]=$$

$$\left[\frac{6}{2}+\frac{1}{2}\right]-\left[\frac{10}{5}+\frac{3}{5}\right]=$$

$$\frac{7}{2}-\frac{13}{5}=$$

Then find the lowest common denominator.

$$\frac{7}{2}-\frac{13}{5}=$$

$$\left(\frac{7}{2}\times\frac{5}{5}\right)-\left(\frac{13}{5}\times\frac{2}{2}\right)=$$

$$\frac{35}{10}-\frac{26}{10}=$$

$$\frac{9}{10}$$

14) The correct answer is B. Remember for division of fractions, you need to invert the second fraction and then multiply the fractions. When you multiply fractions, you multiply the numerators with each other for the new numerator, and the denominators with each other for the new denominator. For problems like this, deal with the parts of the equation in the parentheses first.

$$\frac{1}{6}+\left(\frac{1}{2}\div\frac{3}{8}\right)-\left(\frac{1}{3}\times\frac{3}{2}\right)=$$

$$\frac{1}{6}+\left(\frac{1}{2}\times\frac{8}{3}\right)-\left(\frac{1}{3}\times\frac{3}{2}\right)=$$

$$\frac{1}{6}+\frac{8}{6}-\frac{3}{6}$$

After you have done the operations on the parentheses, you can add and subtract as needed.

$$\frac{1}{6}+\frac{8}{6}-\frac{3}{6}=$$

$$\frac{9}{6}-\frac{3}{6}=\frac{6}{6}$$

$$\frac{6}{6}=1$$

15) The correct answer is D. We know that Mary has already gotten 80% of the money. However, the question is asking how much money she still needs: 100% – 80% = 20% = .20
Now do the multiplication: 650 × .20 = 130

16) The correct answer is B. Your equation is: (A × \$5) + (B × \$8) = \$60
They buy 4 of product A, so put that in the equation and solve it.
(A × \$5) + (B × \$8) = \$60
(4 × \$5) + (B × \$8) = \$60
\$20 + (B × \$8) = \$60
(B × \$8) = \$40
B = 5

17) The correct answer is C. Remember to assign a different variable to each item. Then make your equation by multiplying each variable by its price. So, let's say that the number of pairs of socks is *S* and the number of pairs of shoes is *H*.
Your equation is: (*S* × \$2) + (*H* × \$25) = \$85
We know that the number of pairs of shoes is 3, so put that in the equation and solve it.
(*S* × \$2) + (*H* × \$25) = \$85
(*S* × \$2) + (3 × \$25) = \$85
(*S* × \$2) + \$75 = \$85
(*S* × \$2) + 75 – 75 = \$85 – \$75

$(S \times \$2) = \$10$
$\$2S = \$10$
$\$2S \div 2 = \$10 \div 2$
$S = 5$
So, she bought 5 pairs of socks.

18) The correct answer is C. To solve inequalities like this one, you should first solve the inequality for x.
$x - 6 < 0$
$x - 6 + 6 < 0 + 6$
$x < 6$
Now solve for y by replacing x with its value.
$y < x + 12$
$y < 6 + 12$
$y < 18$

19) The correct answer is B. Our problem asked for the solution of $2 + y < -8$. Isolate y in order to solve the problem.
$2 + y < -8$
$2 - 2 + y < -8 - 2$
$y < -10$

20) The correct answer is C. Any non-zero number to the power of zero is equal to 1. $(6y)^0 = 1$

21) The correct answer is C. First do the multiplication of the integers. Remember that when there are exponents inside the radical signs, you add the exponents together. So, multiply the integers and add the exponents.

$$\sqrt{14x^5} \times \sqrt{6x^3} = \sqrt{84x^8}$$

Then factor the integer inside the square root sign and simplify. Remember that if you are finding factors for integers inside a radical, you should look for factors are perfect squares. 4 is the only factor of 84 that is a perfect square because the square root of 4 is 2. So, we factor as follows:

$$\sqrt{84x^8} = \sqrt{4 \times 21x^8}$$

Then we simplify like this:

$$\sqrt{4 \times 21x^8} =$$

$$\sqrt{(2 \times 2) \times 21x^8} = 2\sqrt{21x^8}$$

In order to simplify further, we need to deal with the x term. Remember that the square root of any number is that number to the ½ power.

For example, $\sqrt{x} = x^{\frac{1}{2}}$

So, we can further simplify the x term in our problem.

$2\sqrt{21x^8} =$

$2 \times \sqrt{21} \times x^{\frac{8}{2}}$

$2 \times \sqrt{21} \times x^4$

$2x^4\sqrt{21}$

22) The correct answer is A. Remember to multiply the integers, but to add the exponents. Also remember that any variable times itself is equal to that variable squared.
For example, a × a = a^2

$8ab^2(3ab^4 + 2b) =$

$(8ab^2 \times 3ab^4) + (8ab^2 \times 2b) =$

$24a^2b^6 + 16ab^3$

23) The correct answer is D. First you have to find the lowest common denominator (LCD). For denominators that have integers and variables, you need two steps in order to find the LCD. (1) Deal with the integers in the denominator; (2) Then deal with the variable. In order to find the LCD, ask yourself: What is the smallest possible number that is divisible by both 12 and by 10? The answer is 60. Alternatively, find the factors of 12 and 10, and then multiply by the factor that they do not have in common.12 = 2 × 6 and 10 = 2 × 5, so multiply 12 by 5 and 10 by 6 to arrive at 60 for the integer part of the denominator.

Then deal with the variable. $x = x \times 1$ and $x^2 = x \times x$, so multiply $x^2 \times 1$ and $x \times x$, to get x^2 for the variable part of the denominator.

Then put together the product of the LCD for the integer and the product of the LCD for the variable.
60 for the integer
x^2 for the variable

So, the LCD is $60x^2$.

$\frac{5}{12x} + \frac{4}{10x^2} =$

$\left(\frac{5}{12x} \times \frac{5x}{5x}\right) + \left(\frac{4}{10x^2} \times \frac{6}{6}\right) =$

$\frac{25x}{60x^2} + \frac{24}{60x^2} =$

$\frac{25x + 24}{60x^2}$

24) The correct answer is C. To answer this type of question, remember that $x^{-b} = \frac{1}{x^b}$

Therefore, $-5^{-2} = \frac{1}{-5^2} = \frac{1}{25}$

25) The correct answer is A. In order to solve by elimination, you need to subtract the second equation from the first equation. Look at the term containing *x* in the second equation. We have 8*x* in the second equation. In order to eliminate the term containing *x*, we need to multiply the first equation by 8.

$x + 5y = 24$

$(8 \times x) + (5y \times 8) = (24 \times 8)$

$8x + 40y = 192$

Now do the subtraction.

$$\begin{array}{r} 8x + 40y = 192 \\ -(8x + 2y = 40) \\ \hline 38y = 152 \end{array}$$

Then solve for y.

$38y = 152$

$38y \div 38 = 152 \div 38$

$y = 4$

Now put the value for *y* into the first equation and solve for *x*.

$x + 5y = 24$

$x + (5 \times 4) = 24$

$x + 20 = 24$

$x + 20 - 20 = 24 - 20$

$x = 4$

$x = 4$ and $y = 4$, so the answer is (4, 4).

26) The correct answer is C. For problems like this one, you need to multiply the first term in the first set of parentheses by all of the terms in the second set of parentheses. Then multiply the second term in the first set of parentheses by all of the terms in the second set of parentheses. So, you need to multiply as shown.

$(4x - 3)(5x^2 + 12x + 11) =$

$[(4x \times 5x^2) + (4x \times 12x) + (4x \times 11)] - [(3 \times 5x^2) + (3 \times 12x) + (3 \times 11)] =$

$(20x^3 + 48x^2 + 44x) - (15x^2 + 36x + 33)$

Then simplify, remembering to be careful about the negative sign in front of the second set of parentheses.

$(20x^3 + 48x^2 + 44x) - (15x^2 + 36x + 33) =$

$(20x^3 + 48x^2 + 44x) - 15x^2 - 36x - 33 =$

$20x^3 + 48x^2 - 15x^2 + 44x - 36x - 33 =$

$20x^3 + 33x^2 + 8x - 33$

27) The correct answer is C. Remember to multiply the integers inside the two radical signs and add the exponents when multiplying the two terms.

$\sqrt{6x^3}\sqrt{24x^5} =$

$\sqrt{144x^8}$

Then find the square root, if possible.

$\sqrt{144x^8} =$

$\sqrt{(12 \times 12)(x^4 \times x^4)} =$

$12x^4$

28) The correct answer is B. Factor the integers inside each of the square root signs. Remember that you need to find a perfect square for one of the factors for each radical.

$\sqrt{18} + 3\sqrt{32} + 5\sqrt{8} =$

$\sqrt{2 \times 9} + 3\sqrt{2 \times 16} + 5\sqrt{2 \times 4} =$

$\sqrt{2 \times (3 \times 3)} + 3\sqrt{2 \times (4 \times 4)} + 5\sqrt{2 \times (2 \times 2)} =$

$3\sqrt{2} + (3 \times 4)\sqrt{2} + (5 \times 2)\sqrt{2}$

Then do the multiplication and addition.

$3\sqrt{2} + (3 \times 4)\sqrt{2} + (5 \times 2)\sqrt{2} =$

$3\sqrt{2} + 12\sqrt{2} + 10\sqrt{2} =$

$(3 + 12 + 10)\sqrt{2} =$

$25\sqrt{2}$

29) The correct answer is D. When you have fractions in the numerator and denominator of another fraction, you can divide the two fractions as shown.

$$\frac{\frac{5a}{b}}{\frac{2a}{a-b}} = \frac{5a}{b} \div \frac{2a}{a-b}$$

Then invert and multiply just like you would for any other fraction.

$$\frac{5a}{b} \div \frac{2a}{a-b} =$$

$$\frac{5a}{b} \times \frac{a-b}{2a} =$$

$$\frac{5a^2 - 5ab}{2ab}$$

Then simplify, if possible.

$$\frac{5a^2 - 5ab}{2ab} =$$

$$\frac{a(5a-5b)}{a(2b)} =$$

$$\frac{5a-5b}{2b}$$

30) The correct answer is D. Find the lowest common denominator.

$$\frac{1}{a+1} + \frac{1}{a} =$$

$$\left(\frac{1}{a+1} \times \frac{a}{a}\right) + \left(\frac{1}{a} \times \frac{a+1}{a+1}\right) =$$

$$\frac{a}{a^2+a} + \frac{a+1}{a^2+a}$$

Then simplify, if possible

$$\frac{a}{a^2+a} + \frac{a+1}{a^2+a} =$$

$$\frac{a+a+1}{a^2+a} =$$

$$\frac{2a+1}{a^2+a}$$

31) The correct answer is C. You will remember that the slope intercept formula is: $y = mx + b$

Remember that *m* is the slope and *b* is the *y* intercept. You will also need the slope formula:

$$m = \frac{y_2 - y_1}{x_2 - x_1}$$

We are given the slope, as well as the point (4,5), so first we need to put those points into the slope formula. We are doing this in order to solve for *b*, which is not provided in the facts of the problem.

$$\frac{y_2 - y_1}{x_2 - x_1} = -\frac{3}{5}$$

$$\frac{5 - y_1}{4 - x_1} = -\frac{3}{5}$$

Then eliminate the denominator.

$$(4 - x_1)\frac{5 - y_1}{4 - x_1} = -\frac{3}{5}(4 - x_1)$$

$$5 - y_1 = -\frac{3}{5}(4 - x_1)$$

Now put in 0 for x_1 in the slope formula in order to find *b*, which is the *y* intercept (the point at which the line crosses the *y* axis).

$$5 - y_1 = -\frac{3}{5}(4 - x_1)$$

$$5 - y_1 = -\frac{3}{5}(4 - 0)$$

$$5 - y_1 = -\frac{3 \times 4}{5}$$

$$5 - y_1 = -\frac{12}{5}$$

$$5 - 5 - y_1 = -\frac{12}{5} - 5$$

$$-y_1 = -\frac{12}{5} - 5$$

$$-y_1 \times -1 = \left(-\frac{12}{5} - 5\right) \times -1$$

$$y_1 = \frac{12}{5} + 5$$

$$y_1 = \frac{12}{5} + \left(5 \times \frac{5}{5}\right)$$

$$y_1 = \frac{12}{5} + \frac{25}{5}$$

$$y_1 = \frac{12+25}{5}$$

$$y_1 = \frac{37}{5}$$

Remember that the *y* intercept (known in the slope-intercept formula as the variable *b*) exists when *x* is equal to 0.

We have put in the value of 0 for *x* in the equation above, so $b = \frac{37}{5}$

Now put the value for *b* into the slope intercept formula.

$y = mx + b$

$$y = -\frac{3}{5}x + \frac{37}{5}$$

32) The correct answer is D. Use the midpoint formula. For two points on a graph (x_1, y_1) and (x_2, y_2), the midpoint is: $(x_1 + x_2) \div 2$, $(y_1 + y_2) \div 2$
$(2 + 4) \div 2$ = midpoint *x*, $(2 - 6) \div 2$ = midpoint *y*
$6 \div 2$ = midpoint *x*, $-4 \div 2$ = midpoint *y*
3 = midpoint *x*, –2 = midpoint *y*

33) The correct answer is A. Use the distance formula.

$$d = \sqrt{(x_2 - x_1)^2 + (y_2 - y_1)^2}$$

Now we need to put in the values stated: $(3\sqrt{3}, -1)$ and $(6\sqrt{3}, 2)$

$$d = \sqrt{(6\sqrt{3} - 3\sqrt{3})^2 + (2 - -1)^2}$$

$$d = \sqrt{(3\sqrt{3})^2 + (3)^2}$$

$$d = \sqrt{(9 \times 3) + 9}$$

$$d = \sqrt{27 + 9}$$

$$d = \sqrt{36}$$

$$d = 6$$

34) The correct answer is A. The perimeter of a rectangle is equal to two times the length plus two times the width. We can express this concept as an equation: P = 2L + 2W
Now set up formulas for the perimeters both before and after the increase.

STEP 1 – Before the increase:
$P = 2L + 2W$
$48 = 2L + 2W$
$48 \div 2 = (2L + 2W) \div 2$
$24 = L + W$
$24 - W = L + W - W$
$24 - W = L$

STEP 2 – After the increase (width is increased by 5 and length is doubled):
$P = 2L + 2W$
$92 = (2 \times 2)L + 2(W + 5)$
$92 = 4L + 2W + 10$
$92 - 10 = 4L + 2W + 10 - 10$
$82 = 4L + 2W$

Then solve by substitution. In this case, we substitute 24 – W (which we calculated in the "before" equation in step 1) for L in the "after" equation calculated in step 2, in order to solve for W.
$82 = 4L + 2W$
$82 = 4(24 - W) + 2W$
$82 = 96 - 4W + 2W$
$82 - 96 = 96 - 96 - 4W + 2W$
$-14 = -2W$
$7 = W$

Then substitute the value for W in order to solve for L.
$24 - W = L$
$24 - 7 = L$
$17 = L$

35) The correct answer is D. The area of a circle is always π times the radius squared. Therefore, the area of circle A is: $3^2\pi = 9\pi$. Since the circles are internally tangent, the radius of circle B is calculated by taking the radius of circle A times 2. In other words, the diameter of circle A is the radius of circle B. Therefore, the radius of circle B is $3 \times 2 = 6$ and the area of circle B is $6^2\pi = 36\pi$. To calculate the remaining area of circle B, we subtract as follows: $36\pi - 9\pi = 27\pi$

36) The correct answer is C. Remember that the perimeter is the measurement along the outside edge of a geometrical figure. Since the figure in this problem is a square, we know that the four sides are equal in length. To find the length of one side, we therefore divide the perimeter by four: $24 \div 4 = 6$

Now we use the Pythagorean Theorem to find the length of line segment AB. Remember that the Pythagorean Theorem states that the length of the hypotenuse is equal to the square root of the sum of the squares of the two other sides. The hypotenuse is the part of a triangle that is opposite to the right angle, so in this case AB is the hypotenuse. The hypotenuse length is the square root of $6^2 + 6^2$.

$\sqrt{6^2 + 6^2} =$

$\sqrt{36 + 36} = \sqrt{72}$

So, the answer is $\sqrt{72}$.

37) The correct answer is C. The circumference of a circle is always calculated by using this formula: Circumference = π × diameter
The diameter of a circle is always equal to the radius times 2.
So, the diameter for this circle is 4 × 2 = 8.
Therefore, the circumference is 8π.

38) The correct answer is D.
Area of a circle = π × radius^2
The radius of this circle is 6.
$6^2 = 36$
Therefore, the area is 36π.

39) The correct answer is B.
The area of circle A is $0.4^2\pi = 0.16\pi$
The area of circle B is $0.2^2\pi = 0.04\pi$
Then subtract: $0.16\pi - 0.04\pi = 0.12\pi$

40) The correct answer is D. The volume of a box is calculated by taking the length times the width times the height: 5 × 6 × 10 = 300

41) The correct answer is C. The length of the hypotenuse is always the square root of the sum of the squares of the other two sides of the triangle:
L = $\sqrt{M^2 + N^2}$
Now put in the values for the above problem.
L = $\sqrt{M^2 + N^2}$
L = $\sqrt{3^2 + 2^2}$
L = $\sqrt{9 + 4}$
L = $\sqrt{13}$

42) The correct answer is B. Triangle area = (base × height) ÷ 2
Substitute the amounts for base and height: area = (5 × 2) ÷ 2 = 10 ÷ 2 = 5

43) The correct answer is B. Hypotenuse length C = $\sqrt{A^2 + B^2}$

$\sqrt{34} = \sqrt{25 + B^2}$

$B^2 = 9$

$B = 3$

44) The correct answer is A. To solve this problem, remember these three principles:
(1) Arc length is the distance on the outside (or circumference) of a circle.
(2) The circumference of a circle is always π times the diameter.
(3) There are 360 degrees in a circle.
The angle in this problem is 30 degrees.
$360 \div 30 = 12$
In other words, we are dealing with the circumference of $^{1}/_{12}$ of the circle.
Given that the circumference of this circle is 12π, and we are dealing only with $^{1}/_{12}$ of the circle, then the arc length for this angle is: $12\pi \div 12 = \pi$

45) The correct answer is B. Cone volume = $(\pi \times \text{radius}^2 \times \text{height}) \div 3$
Substitute the values for base and height.
volume = $(\pi 3^2 \times 4) \div 3 =$
$(\pi 9 \times 4) \div 3 =$
$\pi 36 \div 3 = 12\pi$

46) The correct answer is B. Remember that the perimeter is the measurement along the outside edges of the rectangle or other area. The formula for perimeter is as follows:
P = 2W + 2L

If the room is 12 feet by 10 feet, we need 12 feet × 2 feet to finish the long sides of the room and 10 feet × 2 feet to finish the shorter sides of the room.
$(2 \times 10) + (2 \times 12) =$
$20 + 24 = 44$

47) The correct answer is A. First, we have to calculate the total square footage available.
If there are 4 rooms which are 10 by 10 each, we have this equation:
$4 \times (10 \times 10) = 400$ square feet in total

Now calculate the square footage of the new rooms.
$20 \times 10 = 200$
2 rooms × $(10 \times 8) = 160$
$200 + 160 = 360$ total square feet for the new rooms

So, the remaining square footage for the bathroom is calculated by taking the total minus the square footage of the new rooms.
$400 - 360 = 40$ square feet
Since each existing room is 10 feet long, we know that the new bathroom also needs to be 10 feet long in order to fit in. So, the new bathroom is 4 feet × 10 feet.

48) The correct answer is D. First, calculate the area of the central rectangle. Remember that the area of a rectangle is length times height: $8 \times 3 = 24$
Using the Pythagorean Theorem, we know that the base of each triangle is 4.
$5 = \sqrt{3^2 + base^2}$
$5^2 = 3^2 + \text{base}^2$

$25 = 9 + \text{base}^2$
$25 - 9 = 9 - 9 + \text{base}^2$
$16 = \text{base}^2$
$4 = \text{base}$

Then calculate the area of each of the triangles on each side of the central rectangle. Remember that the area of a triangle is base times height divided by 2: $(4 \times 3) \div 2 = 6$

So, the total area is the area of the main rectangle plus the area of each of the two triangles.
$24 + 6 + 6 = 36$

49) The correct answer is B. Remember that the area of a triangle is base times height divided by 2. First, calculate the area of triangle NKM.
$[6 \times (8 + 10)] \div 2 =$
$(6 \times 18) \div 2 =$
$108 \div 2 = 54$

Then, calculate the area of the area of triangle NKL.
$(6 \times 8) \div 2 = 24$

The remaining triangle NLM is then calculated by subtracting the area of triangle NKL from triangle NKM: $54 - 24 = 30$

50) The correct answer is B. We know that any straight line is 180°. We also know that the sum of the degrees of the three angles of any triangle is 180°. The sum of angles X, Y, and Z = 180. So, the sum of angle X and angle Z equals $180° - 30° = 150°$. Remember that in an isosceles triangle, the angles at the base of the triangle are equal. Because this triangle is isosceles, angle X and angle Z are equivalent. So, we can divide the remaining degrees by 2 as follows: $150° \div 2 = 75°$ In other words, angle X and angle Z are each 75°. Then we need to subtract the degree of the angle $\angle X$ from 180° to get the measurement of $\angle WXY$. $180° - 75° = 105°$

Printed in the USA
CPSIA information can be obtained
at www.ICGtesting.com
LVHW081157181023
761376LV00012B/230

9 780999 808719